DARE
TO
JOURNEY

— WITH —

Henri
Nouwen

D1020382

DARE
TO
JOURNEY
— WITH —

Henri Nouwen

CHARLES RINGMA

PIÑON PRESS

P.O. Box 35007, Colorado Springs, Colorado 80935

Our Guarantee to You

We believe so strongly in the message of our books that we are making this quality guarantee to you. If for any reason you are disappointed with the content of this book, return the title page to us with your name and address and we will refund to you the list price of the book. To help us serve you better, please briefly describe why you were disappointed. Mail your refund request to: PiñonPress, P.O. Box 35002, Colorado Springs, CO 80935.

ISBN 1-57683-226-0

Cover photograph: Derek Gardner/Stone
Cover designer: Dan Jamison
Creative team: Amy Spencer, Darla Hightower, Heather Nordyke

This publication is designed to provide accurate and authoritative information in regard to the subject matter covered. It is sold with the understanding that the author and the publisher are not engaged in rendering legal, accounting, or other professional service. If legal advice or other expert assistance is required, the services of a competent professional person should be sought. *From a Declaration of Principles jointly adopted by a Committee of the American Bar Association and a Committee of Publishers.*

Library of Congress Cataloging-in-Publication Data

Ringma, Charles.
    Dare to journey with Henri Nouwen / Charles Ringma.
        p. cm.
    Includes bibliographical references and index.
    ISBN 1-57683-226-0
        1. Nouwen, Henri J. M. I. Title.

BX4705.N87 R56 2000
248.4'82—dc21

00-062490

Printed in the United States of America

3 4 5 6 7 8 9 10 11 12 13 14 / 09 08 07 06 05 04 03 02

Dedication

For the one who has given me
true companionship, much warmth,
persistent encouragement and
gentle but firm challenge—
Rita

CONTENTS

PREFACE

I HAVE WRITTEN THIS BOOK BECAUSE I BELIEVE THAT there is an intimate connection between personal well-being and the development of the inner life. Our culture is not rich in understanding the development of spirituality. It tends to be too pragmatically focused. The issue for our culture is what we produce and achieve, not what we are.

Our religious institutions often fail to aid us in our spiritual development. They provide rituals, symbols, doctrines, and meetings, but they often don't help us to move to the experiential and practical. They may tell us that we should pray but do not teach us how to pray.

Dare to Journey with Henri Nouwen attempts to bring us to the "how" of the development of the spiritual life without resorting to techniques. It sets out a pattern of inner development that moves us from where we are to a place of refreshment so that we can purposefully reengage the issues we need to face in our world. It seeks to do this not by doctrines or rituals, but by a wisdom born of life experience.

This work is designed to be used as a handbook for personal inner development, reflection, and meditation, for times of retreat, spiritual renewal, reevaluation, and prayer. It is meant to be a conversation partner, not a book of answers. *Dare to Journey* seeks to encourage its readers in the journey that each of us must make, without providing all the road maps.

My special thanks go to Karen McColm for typing the manuscript, to my friends at Jubilee Fellowship for their encouragement and feedback, and to Helen Woolcock for many helpful comments on the content and style of this book.

—CHARLES RINGMA
Brisbane, Australia, 1991

INTRODUCTION

THERE ARE SEASONS IN THE SPIRITUAL LIFE: THE MOVE-
ment from immaturity to maturity, the journey from
struggle to surrender, the path of turmoil to peace, faith
to understanding, and sowing to reaping.

But there is a problem with a linear projection of
the inner life where we move from one plateau to the
next, from one state of existence to another. Life is just
not like this. It is more circular. There are times when,
as it were, we have to start all over again, when we have
to be converted again and to relearn lessons and disciplines that we have neglected in our spiritual
formation.

At the same time, we experience life as paradox-
ical. Things stand in tension with each other, and
things do not always work out in anticipated ways.
Good sometimes has unfortunate consequences, and
out of tragedy blessings can emerge. Thus the spiritual journey does not consist of neat stages. Seldom
do we move smoothly from "darkness" to "enlight-
enment" and live happily ever after in the latter state.

In this collection of reflections and meditations,
we prefer to speak of the rhythms of the spiritual life,
the to-and-fro movement that not only calls us forward, but also calls us to retreat. This approach
recognizes that ecstasy and despair, inwardness and
worldly concern, maturity and simplicity, growth and
conversion, spiritual power and repentance, faith
and fear, loneliness and friendship all jostle together

as we seek to grow in the spiritual disciplines.

One of the most basic rhythms of the inner life is the movement from our restless senses to an inner solitude in order to reengage the world with new creativity and hope. It is the movement from where we are—with our struggles, burdens, and pains—in order to drink again at the fountain of life, the place of God's encouragement where we can find inner renewal for our ongoing participation in our world.

The rhythm starts with where we are, not idealistically with where we think we ought to be. It helps us to focus realistically on what is happening to us. It looks life squarely in the face and makes no excuses.

The second stage in this rhythm occurs when we are drawn to the place of solitude and the source of renewal. This is the place where we lay down our burdens, confess our failures, lance our hurts, expose our grief, and acknowledge our foolishness and idolatry. This place is God's loving presence, where we can be embraced, forgiven, empowered, and fueled for the journey.

The third stage in the rhythm is when we can reengage our circumstances and our world with these new resources and creativity so that we are no longer overwhelmed, but are able to respond with newfound courage.

If we don't start with the first stage, we live in unreality. If we don't move to the second stage, we may end up living in despair and will certainly exhaust our inner resources. If, however, we fail to engage in the third stage, we may be spiritually replete, but we are socially irrelevant.

In the particular way that these reflections have been grouped together, this rhythm of the spiritual life will become all the more apparent. To help in this journey of discovery, we have invited Henri Nouwen to join us. A well-known Catholic writer on spirituality, Nouwen demonstrates a sensitive intimacy in the quest for wholeness. This will complement our own struggle toward the light and our groping for faith and authenticity in a secularized world.

This world is to be my home, as much as it is not to be the place that sets the agenda for my life. It is the place that sustains me, but that also needs to be transformed by the grace of God. Thus, while participating in all of life, I need to draw aside to find a place of intimacy with the God who loves and sustains me. And from this reoccurring center-point I can be personally enriched so that I can continue to wash the feet of the world.

Wasted Time:

Taking Time for Inner Renewal

There is just so much that needs to be done. Extra demands at home and at work. More time with the family. Keeping up with our exercise program. Planning the next holiday. Time out for friends. Involvement in our children's school activities. Completing that new management course.

In these and many other ways, the busy round of life draws us into a myriad of activities, all important, but all demanding more of our time and energy. Even church activities jostle for our attention and commitment. And creative acts of service requiring long-term support and care often demand more than we are able to give.

So we try to do more while our energies ebb away and we become like uprooted trees with our roots wildly groping for the sky. Thus we anxiously throw our arms toward heaven, praying for extra grace and special enabling, when instead we should be planted again in nourishing soil. That soil is not meant to make us do less, but to change our priorities so that we take time to be still. And in the stillness, find new strength and hope.

Henri Nouwen reminds us that "time given to inner renewal is never wasted."[1] In fact it is the fuel for the journey, and more importantly, it is the discipline that will shape the very fabric of our being.

Loneliness:

The Surprising Way to a New Openness

We are often afraid to be alone. Afraid of what we may discover about ourselves when we stop long enough to be still. Afraid of the insecurities and sins that still lurk within us even though we have tried so hard to sublimate them. Afraid to face our insignificance, lack of fulfillment, and the eventuality of our death. And afraid to face the lack of closure and resolution of issues that we have tried so hard to square away.

Yet we need to be alone. For we need to rediscover ourselves as much as we need to bask in the searchlight of God's love and light—to face our pain and lack of resolution with new hope and faith. In learning to be alone and still, we make a way to meet God with openness and honesty. It is there we can rediscover that we cannot blame others or live in unreality.

Nouwen speaks of the importance of experiencing a loneliness "that cannot be removed by any other sinful human being."[2] For it is not to others that we should first of all turn; instead, we should create the necessary space to meet with God Himself. While we may fear this place of quietness and openness, it is the only road that will lead to new life. For from new insights come new motivations, which give us new strength, and this will only come when we are loved, sheltered, and affirmed, as well as corrected by the One who truly knows and loves us.

From Restlessness to Solitude:

Finding a New Center

We need to learn to face ourselves and come to acknowledge our inner pain and frustrations. More importantly, in the loneliness of who we are, we need to recognize our powerlessness to achieve the good and to control our own existence. While we are to act decisively and to be responsible for our own choices, we need to recognize that we are not the masters of our own fate.

These insights need not drive us to despair, but to a new acknowledgment of our creatureliness and of our need to come into a relationship with God where our strivings are transformed into a new sense of trust.

Nouwen speaks of the movement "from the restless senses to the restful spirit."[3] Such a movement is not an attempt to escape from ourselves, but the bringing of ourselves to find a new center. Nor is such a movement simply an attempt to escape the pressures of our world. This is no more than a dream and an illusion. Instead, this movement is the bringing of our whole selves, with all our fears and pain, to find a new center of inner peace.

This can begin to be found when we meet with the God who does not necessarily relieve us of our burdens nor answer all our concerns, but who embraces us so that our burdens become light on our journey ahead.

Prayer:

An Invitation to Be Loved and Nurtured

Much of our praying is asking because there is so much that we think we need. Some of our praying is frantic because we are in difficult circumstances. Sometimes our praying is manipulative because we assume that we know better than God what we need and what must take place.

But prayer is meant to be something quite different. It is an invitation to come home, to be loved, nurtured, and refreshed. Nouwen puts it this way: "Praying . . . demands a relationship in which you allow the other to speak there, allow him to touch the sensitive core of your being, and allow him to see so much that you would rather leave in darkness."[4]

Prayer is thus the call to intimacy with the God of the universe, who is our Father in Jesus Christ. Prayer is listening to what He would whisper to us. Prayer is being renewed by His loving presence. Prayer is being exposed, embraced, and healed by Him who alone knows what is best for us.

Hearing:

Being in the Place to Find New Directions

One of our biggest challenges is to resist doing more. It is to be still long enough to evaluate our many activities. Activities that drive us to distraction and sometimes exhaustion, but also give us meaning and fulfillment. Activities that can give us our routines and our security, but can also block out the "voice" of correction and change.

We need to recognize that all our much-doing is not always fruitful. It is sometimes mindless. Sometimes it is driven. It can be self-protecting. It keeps us going when in fact we should be still—still in order to evaluate and to hear.

Thus a far greater challenge is not to do, but to be in the place where we can hear; not to hear the old and familiar, but to hear again what God thinks about our life's direction, priorities, and activities—and to hear again what our heart is saying. This is often difficult for us. It is a struggle.

Nouwen writes about learning to listen "carefully to the inner movements of the spirit and struggling with the question 'How do I follow Jesus all the way?'"[5] This is the struggle to hear what we may not wish to hear. It is a groping toward an openness that may cause our life to be turned around.

Yet hear new things we must! For we cannot simply continue to plunge headlong into the incessant round of activities that are no longer a part of God's direction for our lives and that no longer express our creativity and our central concerns.

God's Unlikely Spokespersons:

Hearing God's Voice Through Others

God has an immense sense of humor. This is not a negative reflection on His holiness and majesty, but a recognition of the amazing way He works in human affairs. Simply stated, He is seldom impressed with our definitions of what is important.

God tends not to recognize our stereotyped explanations of the way we think that God should act. In the past, He chose a mere shepherd in the form of Amos to be His spokesperson, used the pagan King Cyrus to execute His justice, called a maiden to give birth to His Son, and used fishermen to establish His church. Nouwen observes that "the most unlikely people are chosen by God to make us see."[6]

Sadly, we frequently fail to hear God's unlikely mouthpieces, for we regard them as socially unacceptable and therefore as not credible and worthy of our attention. Yet, from someone young in the faith we can hear wisdom, from secular prophets we hear legitimate criticism of the church, from the poor we hear God's cry for justice, and from those who have suffered much we can frequently hear words of graciousness and forgiveness.

It is therefore important that these voices be heard, including God's unlikely spokespersons, if we wish to hear all that God may want to say to us. The difficulty is usually not a lack of voices, but a discernment to hear what we most urgently need to hear.

From Inner Stillness to Active Engagement:

Finding a New Self to Serve the World

We need to resist making unhelpful distinctions where we play off one thing against another. Prayer, for example, is not opposed to work; and the search for solitude is not opposed to active involvement in our world. These seeming opposites belong together. Prayer leads to work, and work needs to be done prayerfully. Similarly, solitude is not simply a withdrawal from the world in order to be renewed and refreshed. It is also finding a new center of inner quietness and certitude from which we act in the midst of a busy and demanding world.

Nouwen expresses the seeming paradox in this way: "The movement from loneliness to solitude is not a movement of growing withdrawal, but is instead a movement toward a deeper engagement in the burning issues of our time."[7] This seeming contradiction finds its resolution in the fact that we can lose ourselves in our much-doing but cannot find ourselves simply through withdrawal.

In our much-doing we lose perspective, lose our energy, and more importantly, lose our creativity and sense of humor. We thus begin to carry the world on our shoulders and soon become overwhelmed or disillusioned. But to simply withdraw does not provide the way forward, for we then take our hurt or tired self with us. Rather, the movement to solitude is to find a renewed self, and from the center of being loved and nourished we can again enter our world with purposeful engagement and joyful detachment.

Come Home:

Finding a Place of Safety

Every home is not necessarily a haven of peace. Every church is not necessarily a community of love and service. And the workplace is not always a place of cooperation. Nor are all our relationships healing and encouraging. Thus in the midst of life, we can feel lost and alienated.

We therefore need to hear the call to come home, home to the Father's heart. Nouwen states that in prayer, God so much wants "to give a home, a sense of belonging, a place to dwell, a shelter where I feel protected and a refuge in which I feel safe."[8]

This place of safety can be found in our world, but only in the place of prayer—a place of fellowship with the Father of all grace and consolation, who invites me to be with Him. It is there that we are truly at home. And it is from this center that we seek to build families of joy and openness, churches of reconciliation, workplaces of productivity and partnership, and friendships that are not stifling, but are marked by servanthood and reciprocity.

Realistic Expectations:

Avoiding Expecting What Others Cannot Give

We can expect too much of others. This is particularly so when we stand in a meaningful relationship with others. From those we love much we often expect much, and from those we serve well we frequently expect progress and thankfulness. But our expectations may be unrealistic. Families can become ghettos of unfulfilled expectations, and Christians can be hurt when they expect too much from each other in the form of understanding, encouragement, and mutual support.

It is therefore important that we assume the responsibility of reevaluating our expectations of others. One important factor is to ask whether we are at the right address. We can expect something that others may not be able to give. Nouwen warns us against "expecting from a friend what only Christ can give."[9]

A second issue is to look at our motives for service. All too frequently we give in order to get.

Finally, we need to realize that one of the greatest gifts we can give to others is the gift of freedom, where we allow the other person to take the responsibility for his or her own responses, choices, and future.

The Call of the Small:

Many Small Acts Make Us into the People We Are Becoming

Sometimes we are called to do great acts of kindness or make great sacrifices. But this is seldom normal. Usually we have the opportunity for many small acts of love and service and are called to make many small sacrifices. The significance and power of these cannot be underestimated. Nouwen speaks of "the mystery of small acts of faith,"[10] and in so doing, points to the potential inherent in our acts of love.

Some acts of faith produce unexpected results. Others are more predictable, and some, downright disappointing. But all—and herein lies the mystery—weave a pattern for our being, thinking, responding, and acting. This pattern thus becomes an expression of our truer self. It makes us what we want to be.

Equally importantly, this pattern of many small acts of faith and love weaves an environment of care and consistency for those for whom we are concerned and seek to serve. In being responded to with a persistent love, they can begin to hope and live again.

Drawing Close:

True Compassion Enters the Places of Pain

We are good at criticizing others and even better at giving advice. We assume that we know what is best for others, particularly the more unfortunate members of our society. But we are not so good at compassionate participation. We often fail to draw close. We are afraid of involvement, for we know that we may not be able to control the demands that may be made of us.

Yet compassion asks us precisely to take such a risk. In the words of Nouwen, "compassion asks us to go where it hurts, to enter into places of pain."[11]

Going there does not mean barging in with easy answers and quick solutions. It means learning to listen even for what, initially, cannot be expressed. It means being honest about our own needs and struggles so that we can listen more carefully. It means journeying with people in their attempts at resolution and healing. It means being there, but not controlling or crowding others. It means reaching out without taking over. It means holding without withholding, giving without looking to receive, and entering a partnership that releases others to pursue their own dreams and aspirations.

In the Lonely Place:

Learning to Face the Hard Issues

We seldom make important personal decisions while caught up in the hectic pace of life. And God seldom seems to speak to us about the big issues of our life or life's purpose and direction while we are preoccupied with our everyday affairs. It is usually in the quieter moments of our existence that we can sense new stirrings within us, new longings, and the often vague unfolding of new dreams.

It is also in the lonely place that we can begin to tackle the hard and difficult issues that we need to face but so frequently suppress because of our cluttered life and our reluctance to be open to change. Nouwen reminds us that "in the lonely place Jesus finds the courage to follow God's will."[12]

But it is never the lonely place itself that helps us find new purpose and hope. The lonely place can be the place of fear and despair. Quietness of itself does not produce insight, and solitude as such does not provide new energies. It is what we bring to the lonely place that determines its outcome. If we bring the searching heart, we will find. If we come acknowledging our timidity, we will gain new courage. If we come looking for new direction, we will find a new purpose. If we come admitting our brokenness but longing for healing, admitting our confusion but seeking God's peace, then in the lonely place we will surely be found by Him who seeks us out in love.

Too Full:

Learning to Become Empty

It may come as a shock, but we are often too full of ourselves, too preoccupied with our own activities, and too full of our own plans and desires. Even our activities on behalf of others can often reflect much of our own need for fulfillment or recognition. And our relationship with God frequently pivots around our own prayers, needs, and projects. We are therefore persons without space and room, and consequently we lack flexibility and maneuverability.

We therefore need to be, as it were, pried loose from ourselves. Nouwen, in speaking of prayer as a way to solitude, challenges us to be willing to open our tightly clenched fist and "give up [our] last coin."[13] So often we receive nothing from our spiritual exercises because we have not created any open spaces in our lives. We are too full. We may want to receive, but we certainly do not want anything to be taken away.

God can hardly fill our hands with the good things of His love and grace while our hands are full with our own things. Therefore, in our search for inner peace and strength, we need to learn the gentle but difficult art of relinquishment as much as we need to seek God's empowerment.

The Place of Conversion:

Laying Aside Our Own Agendas

One of our persistent difficulties is that while we want help, we do not want to change. We are quite willing to go to God to ask for strength, but not so willing to ask for redirection. We are happy to be encouraged, but not to be converted.

In doing this we are making the fatal assumption that we are okay in what we are doing and in our priorities; all we lack is adequate resources. And so we turn to God in prayer asking for more grace, more of His Spirit, and more of His power. Even in our search for solitude and inner peace, we are frequently motivated by the idea that we are simply looking to find greater inner energies in order to carry on with our own agendas.

Nouwen, however, reminds us that the place of solitude "is not a private therapeutic place . . . it is the place of conversion."[14] It is not the place where we recharge our spiritual batteries and then continue to live as we have lived before. It is not the place where we catch our breath in order to madly reenter the race. It is not the place where we simply find some quietness before we plunge into the world with its babble of voices.

The place of solitude is where we are changed. It is the place where we abandon some of our agendas, where we acknowledge our compulsions, where we discover new directions, and where, more importantly, we find a new self.

Our Restless Senses:

Coming to God As We Are

Most of us can concentrate long enough on a specific task in order to complete it, particularly
when we are pressured by time. But when we are without external constraints, we easily become less focused.
This is especially the case when we set time aside to
pray and to be still. Our restless senses catapult us from
one thing to another.

Nouwen describes one aspect of our difficulty
when he writes: "Why should I spend an hour in
prayer when I do nothing during that time but think
about people I am angry with, people who are angry
with me . . . and thousands of other silly things that
happen to grab my mind for a moment?"[15]

The answer may be to adopt various spiritual disciplines and techniques to help focus our thoughts. But
more importantly, our coming to God is not an
attempt to impress Him regarding our disciplinary
skills. Instead, we need to bring ourselves to God as
we are—with our restless senses. When we come in
this way, we will eventually experience God's quieting
presence, particularly when we confess our sins,
unburden our hearts, lay down our issues, and allow
ourselves to be blown in new directions by the breath
of God's Spirit.

A Change of Circumstances or Self:

Facing Our Responsibility

We frequently tell ourselves, *If only my circumstances were different, then things would be a whole lot better.* And so we begin the merry-go-round of wishful thinking: *If only I had a different job . . . If only my child had turned out differently . . . If only I had married someone else . . . If only I had stayed on at school.*

It hardly needs to be said that this approach to our circumstances is less than productive. It blinds us to what is good in our present situation, and it constantly shifts the responsibility regarding what is happening to us "over there."

A far more productive approach is that we own our circumstances as being the result of our own choices and begin to entertain the question: What is God seeking to do in my life through my present circumstances? Nouwen records the advice he received from a fellow priest: "The issue is not where you are, but how you live wherever you are."[16]

Frequently the most relevant issue for us is not a change of circumstances, but a change of self. A change of self does not occur through avoidance behavior. It takes place when we face our excuses and rationalizations and assume responsibility for what we are making of our lives.

An Open Door Opens
New Questions:

Living Without Final Closure

We live with a divided self in a refractory world. Consequently, we are pulled in different directions. And even when we persistently pursue a particular set of goals, often in midstream we want to change direction. Moreover, we achieve certain ambitions, only to realize that those things were not what we really wanted. At the genesis or the culmination of a particular project, or somewhere along the way, we realize that we have not quite got it right. There is more.

So we struggle for new understandings and grope for new directions. This is a perpetual rhythm of our inner being. We are there, but we have not arrived. We are home, but we are still on a journey. We have completed the task, but there is still much that needs to be done.

Nouwen underscores this paradox with the observation that we may gain a new insight, but this will only lead "to many new questions."[17] This means that we need to learn to live without finality and without closure. We are always on the road. Always in flux. Therefore we are always faced with the possibility of growth and the overcoming of our rigid, secure, but inauthentic self.

When "the Less" not "the Much" Is Achieved:

Seeking Genuine Inner Resources

We want to achieve much, but sometimes produce little. This may be particularly the case when we set out to be more patient, loving, caring, and gentle with others. We may well find that the more we try, the less successful we seem to be. Now, clearly there is nothing wrong with our desire to be more constructive and helpful in our relationships with others. But there may well be something wrong with the way we go about these tasks.

One of the least helpful ways is to try to prove something to ourselves. Our attempts to be more loving thus become the spiritual barometer by which we check our rating with God. When we do this, our desire to love others becomes confused with our own needs and our own agenda.

The solution is never to attempt to love others more so that we can feel better about ourselves. This is doing things back to front. The way forward is to know we are loved by God and appreciated by others and, from this center of security, to seek to be more caring and compassionate.

Nouwen notes that "a forgiven person forgives."[18] Equally so, a loved person loves. And a nurtured person cares. The challenge is never simply to try to be more loving, but to seek a deeper inner resource from which our love can flow.

Lack of Resolution:

When Relationships Remain Diffucult

One of the difficulties of life is that we cannot nicely clear everything up. Nouwen admits "that there are still many people with whom I am not fully at peace."[19] And most of us can share his sentiments, for some things do not come to a happy resolution, no matter how hard we have tried. We have prayed for resolution and peace. We have gone to admit our faults and sought forgiveness and reconciliation. We have talked about the issues and confronted the problems, but disharmony, uncertainty, and even distrust continue to linger. The relationship remains refractory, difficult, and ambivalent. And sometimes the harder we try to make things right, the worse it gets.

Frequently the difficulty is that we do not quite know what is really amiss. We are aware of the symptoms, but the ability or the appropriate environment to speak heart-to-heart is lacking. Thus we live with a double pain: lack of insight and openness, and lack of resolution.

This cannot fail to remind us of our own fragility and the brokenness of our world. At such a time, we can only commit these difficult and painful circumstances into the masterful hands of God, awaiting another day and time that will present us with new opportunities to make peace. Such a new opportunity can only be God's gracious gift.

Wounds Are Friends:

The Creative Use of Difficulty

God uses many ways to grab our attention. Usually His way is gently persuasive. He draws us rather than pushes us. He woos rather than commands. He encourages rather than punishes.

But God also creatively uses difficulty to gain our attention. He does not create the difficulty. We are good at doing that; or sometimes the difficulty springs from the brokenness of life itself. But problems can arrest us. And if we are willing to learn from them, they can become our friends.

Nouwen speaks of wounds being "a warning, and paralysis an invitation to search for deeper sources of vitality."[20] We can learn from rejection and disappointment, for they can become the steppingstone to new direction and greater achievement.

But this can occur only if we get our attention off the perpetrators of the things that have upset us. It will take place if we develop a pattern where our problems are used creatively for our inner growth. This can occur not only when we use difficulties to tell us something about ourselves, particularly in the way we respond to them, but also when we use them to search for new responses, new purposes, and new dimensions of grace and forgiveness. For no wound can be so great that it cannot drive us to the source of healing.

Poverty:

Learning to Give Ourselves

We always seem to be better at giving than becoming. We can give love even when we are not intrinsically loving. We can be generous even when we are not truly compassionate. We can be concerned about others and yet essentially still live for ourselves. We can be giving to the poor and yet withhold the very thing they most urgently seek: companionship in the journey.

Nouwen reminds us that "being poor is what Jesus invites us to, and that is much, much harder than serving the poor."[21] If we wish to journey with the poor, we need to become poor ourselves—poor for the sake of the gospel and poor for the sake of our neighbor.

This poverty does not only mean that we voluntarily lay aside our time, our power, and our priorities in order to serve others. At a deeper level, it means that we discover our own poverty, weakness, and brokenness and can thus journey in true companionship with the poor. We journey not as those who have much to give and who have all the answers, but as fellow travelers toward light and liberation.

The Upward Glance:

Being Empowered to Face Our True Self

There is a way of turning to God that is a form of escapism. This occurs when we anxiously pray for divine help and intervention, but fail to face the circumstances that cause our own anxiety. It occurs when we pray to be given a way of escape, but fail to evaluate our own part in our difficulties. It occurs when we look upward, but fail to look inward.

Conversely, there is also a way of looking inward that is less than helpful. This takes place when we turn to find inner peace and inner reserves of nourishment, but instead find confusion and impoverishment. This experience of looking inward drives us to frustration and guilt, for we feel that we have failed.

The basic momentum of the spiritual life is not simply to look inward, nor is it just a matter of looking upward. The momentum is quite different. It is looking upward so that we dare to look inward, and it is looking inward so that we can prayerfully look upward. It is being empowered from above so that we can be honest and realistic with ourselves, and it draws us with our confession and repentance back to God again to receive forgiveness and renewal.

The outcome of this rhythm of the inner life is that we become intimately joined with the One who loves us. We can then join Nouwen in this prayer: "I gradually realise that I want to be seen by you, to dwell under your caring gaze and to grow strong and gentle in your sight."[22]

No Center-Point:

Returning to the Simplicity of Faith

One of our persistent difficulties is that we are always looking to find meaning, purpose, and satisfaction elsewhere than the place where we should be looking. This reflects our restlessness. It also reflects our folly. Having come home, we find it difficult to abide there. Having come to the fountain of life, we fail to drink deeply from its waters. Having found the truth, we look for meaning elsewhere. Nouwen confesses in prayer, "I live as though there were something important to be found outside of you."[23] We find it hard to remain close to the Father's heart. We find it hard to remain on course. The familiar soon loses its appeal for us. We lack an abiding center-point.

So the greatest response that we are frequently called to make is not the call to move forward. It is the call to return—to return to the simplicity of our faith, the generosity of our first love, the willingness to obey, and the intimacy of our relationship with the God who lovingly calls us home. The call to return means that we can only truly live from a center-point in the love and presence of God.

Solitude and Transformation:

Facing the Storm As the Way to Stillness

Solitude is never simply the place of stillness and peace. It also can be the place of initial turmoil. The place where we face ourselves and our pain. The place where we are assailed by our doubts. The place where we see our insignificance and face our lack of wholeness and inner purity. Here the storms rage and the Enemy taunts us to inspire further guilt, fear, and shame. Thus the place of solitude becomes the battleground.

But it also becomes the place of opportunity and transformation. Nouwen reminds us that "solitude is the furnace in which transformation takes place."[24] But this can only take place if the doubts are overcome, the guilt removed, the Enemy expelled, the pain acknowledged, our self-pity surrendered, and our fears stilled.

Solitude is thus the stillness after the storm, the peace after the turmoil. It is not a conforming tranquility that leaves us where we are with our illusions. It is not peace at any price where we suppress the hurting parts of ourselves. It is peace won at the cost of openness and honesty. It is a stillness born of transformation. It is a tranquility as the fruit of forgiveness. It is an inner quietness as a gift from the Great Lover, by whose grace and power we have been carried over the abyss.

Receiving:

Learning to Welcome Another's Gifts

We often think that learning the art of giving is one of our biggest challenges. But giving is relatively easy. While the call to give may at times challenge our selfishness and our priorities, it seldom challenges us radically or deeply. For giving does not expose our own needs; it only calls us to share what we already have. It only calls us to generosity.

Learning the art of receiving, however, is another matter. This calls us to intimacy, honesty, openness, and evaluation. Nouwen reminds us that "Jesus wants us to receive the love that is offered."[25] But this is no easy matter, for to receive the love of another calls me to intimacy. To receive another's love means that my innermost self must be touched. To be loved means that I must bring myself, with my insecurities, pain, and needs, to be embraced by another.

Learning the art of receiving is thus a powerful call to change. For in receiving I need to welcome the other with the gifts that are offered. In receiving I need to make room and space to accept what I frequently fail to realize I need. And in receiving, something is added to me that may bring about change and transformation. Certainly in receiving the love that Jesus offers, I cannot expect to remain the same.

Being and Having:

Resisting Becoming Our Successes

Our successes rather than our failures can become our greatest enemy. This occurs not only when we have to compromise in order to achieve our successes. It occurs more particularly when we become our successes, when our whole life becomes absorbed in what we have achieved and our work merges with the self. As such we will be constantly driven to achieve more. This eventually becomes a destructive force, and we lose ourselves.

Nouwen suggests that in solitude we can "discover that being is more important than having, and that we are worth more than the results of our efforts."[26]

The discovery that I am more important than my work and more important than my successes can be a wonderfully freeing experience. This discovery opens up a space in which I can evaluate, refocus, and be inwardly nourished. In this space I may discover that I need to give more attention to my inner growth, that I need to change aspects of my lifestyle, or that I need to give more attention to those parts of my life that have become neglected.

This discovery will not be without some pain. For to become truer to myself, rather than preoccupied with my successes, will mean learning to live without the intoxication of the praise and affirmation of others.

Them and Us:

Acknowledging What Lurks in the Heart

We have our blind spots. We have our defense mechanisms and an ability to rationalize away personal issues that should require our careful attention. Moreover, we can often see quite clearly what others are doing wrong, but fail to acknowledge our own struggles or our own complicity. We talk about "them" failing to do "this" or wrongly doing "that." We talk about "this" being wrong, with the system, the world, the church, or the workplace. But we fail to acknowledge what lurks in our own hearts and fail to see how we so often contribute to the problem.

Nouwen calls us from this to a "solitude of the heart [where] we can truly listen to the pains of the world because there we can recognise them not as strange and unfamiliar pains, but as pains that are indeed our own."[27] This challenges us not simply to label others' behavior or to condemn. It calls us first of all to draw close, to listen, to discern, to see the factors that contribute to actions of which we don't approve. Moreover, it calls us to look at ourselves. So much of what is wrong with our world, church, and workplace is what is also wrong with us.

This challenges us to both humility and repentance and should express itself in the willingness to stretch out our arms toward other people rather than to inflict our judgment upon them.

The Search for Community:

Vertical Relationships Must Be Maintained

One of our most pressing challenges is to find an inner peace that is not an escape from reality, but is based on doing the will of God. The other is the search for human community. Nouwen reminds us that "we are always in search of a community that can offer us a sense of belonging."[28]

These two searches are closely intertwined, but they are not the same and should never become confused. Our attempts to create the human community should not become a substitute for maintaining our own spiritual journey. We cannot afford to find the group but lose ourselves. Moreover, the warmth of human relationships should not replace an intimacy with the God who calls us into fellowship.

On the other hand, our journey of intimacy with God cannot leave us as solitary persons. God not only calls us to Himself, but also invites us to work out our love and commitment by embracing our companions on the journey, as well as our neighbor who so frequently remains a stranger.

Thus the search for inner peace and empowerment becomes the impulse for a search for human community. Intimacy with God can sustain our efforts at community building. And our attempts at building meaningful human relationships should encourage our need to return to the source of life for nourishment and renewal.

The Old and the New:

Present Good Fuels Future Hope

We do not need to live as if all that we are and have now is all that we will ever be. The present does not need to have the last word. Life always has new possibilities that flow out of new decisions and new commitments. However, we don't always live with a joyful anticipation toward the future. The present can so completely encompass our horizon that we can see nothing else. This is particularly the case when we are discouraged or consumed by our present activities.

Quiet reflection can help to free us from the tyranny of the present. Nevertheless, in our desire for new possibilities and a hope for a better future, we cannot reject the present. We cannot despise or treat lightly what we have now. We cannot reach for the future if we cannot celebrate the good in the present. Nouwen reminds us that "nobody can dream of a new earth when there is no old earth to hold any promises."[29] No one has a hopeful future if the present cannot be affirmed. And those who dream of better things are not those who hate what is now, but who love the present enough to seek its transformation.

When the New Springs Up:

Joy As Sustenance for the Journey

When we create space for ourselves and learn to be still and commune with the God who is at work within our very being, we can begin to hear the voice that can surely guide us. While that voice may affirm the good that we are already doing, it may also call us to take on new challenges. It calls us to embrace new directions. It calls us forward and beyond ourselves.

This may initially be very unsettling. It may even inspire us with fear and trepidation. It will lead us to question whether what we heard was right. It will lead us to struggle and to face the pain of letting go of the old in order to embrace the new.

Yet somewhere in the midst of this turmoil we can come to the peace of certainty. It is this peace that produces the joyful heart—the joyful heart, as Nouwen reminds us, "in which something new is born."[30] This is what sustains us as we live out the vision of the new. This fuels our new sense of calling. This encourages us to overcome the difficulties that stand in our way.

With new directions there must come new enablings. With new demands there must be new energy. With a new vision there must be new hope and new grace. And nothing will empower us to move forward as much as a joyful heart that has heard the call, counted the cost, made its commitment, and embraced the new.

Reluctant obedience or sheer willpower will never last the distance. Only the joyful heart can walk the long and difficult road.

Care:

A Matter of Drawing Close

We cannot simply live for others. A life that is totally focused on others and shows no regard for itself will eventually disintegrate. The idea that such a life is the highest form of spirituality is a misunderstanding of the rhythm of the inner life. That rhythm recognizes that we need to be nurtured, refreshed, and empowered if we are to continue to give.

Yet we cannot live only for ourselves either. The quest for solitude and inner strength can never simply be for that purpose. We are called to serve the world in which we live. Such serving is not simply a matter of techniques. It is also a matter of personal encounter. It is a matter of drawing close. It is a matter of care. Nouwen reminds us that care means to be present to the other person and warns that "cure without care makes us preoccupied with quick changes, impatient and unwilling to share each other's burden."[31]

This warning is well placed. We are usually quick in offering our counseling, healing, and helping strategies, and tend to blame the other for a lack of commitment to our strategies if results are not forthcoming. We find it much more difficult to journey with others, enter their places of pain as they are opened to us, offer friendship even when there is no significant change, and seek to empower rather than help. To do this, we will need to care with a care that springs from being nurtured ourselves.

Where We Want to Be:

The Gift of Perseverance

Our hearts can tell us one thing. Reality often tells us another. Our hearts may desire the good and the beautiful, but our experience of life often falls far short of these ideals. Nouwen observes that "there seems to be a mountain of obstacles preventing people from being where their hearts want to be."[32] Thus we are people who experience a gap. What we hope for is one thing. What we achieve is usually another.

This gap can cause us a great deal of pain. For some, it becomes an intolerable frustration and burden, causing them eventually to discard their hopes and dreams. For some, this experience of the gap leads to total disillusionment and cynicism.

For others, this discrepancy between desires and realization, hopes and fulfillment, plans and achievement is regarded positively. It becomes the means of testing the quality of hopes and the depth of commitment. The delay between the wish and the fulfillment becomes the opportunity to evaluate whether this is really what we are desiring, whether this is worth struggling and working for.

Moreover, the gap starkly reminds us that we alone cannot achieve our own dreams. We need the miracle of God's participation. We need the gift of patience. We need the grace of perseverance. We need to work hard to make things happen, but more urgently, we need God's guidance, sustenance, and help. Thus our experience of the gap can drive us to prayer and humility as well as to persistence and faithfulness.

Letting Go:

Embracing a Little Dying

It is good that we care for what we have. It is good to hold what we have and to carefully maintain what is ours. Possessions and gifts should never be taken lightly or treated with disdain. These things should be productively utilized. Similarly, relationships of love and companionship should be purposefully guarded and ardently maintained. There are, therefore, many important things and values in our lives that we need to hold on to. They need to be guarded.

But there are other things that we need to learn to discard. One of the rhythms of the inner life is to hold to the good and to let go of what is evil, unhelpful, and distracting. Nouwen gently suggests to "open your hands without fear, so the other can blow your sins away."[33]

Yet it is surprising what we hold on to. We prefer the old to the new, the familiar to the unexpected, the predictable to the creative. We hold to old behavior patterns that we know are not very helpful. We maintain the headlong pursuit of goals and objectives that we know will not provide the happiness and fulfillment we seek. We hold on to old hurts and disappointments even though we know that this is poisoning the wells of our inner spirit.

We need to learn to let go, even if it means a little dying. Letting go of the wrong and the unhelpful will alone free us for new possibilities, for it creates an emptiness that can be filled with better things.

Home of the Word:

Hearing the Voice of the Other

Being alone does not mean that we have come to silence and solitude. Much more is required than simply to remove oneself physically from other people. To come to solitude means to come to a productive stillness—a stillness in which, having laid aside our daily cares, we bend our inner ear to listen carefully to our inner voice, the voice that seeks to speak to us beyond the many voices of our anxious, our pragmatic, and our socialized self. Nouwen reminds us that "silence is the home of the word."[34]

But not of any word. For if our solitude is to be productive, then we must not only hear the voice of our anxious or socialized self. We need to hear the other voice. The voice of creativity. The voice of the Spirit. The voice of our hopes and dreams. The voice that gently turns us around and sets us on a better path. The voice that calls us to be truer to our greater aspirations.

In silence and quiet reflection, this other voice can speak with uncanny clarity and certainty. And when this is prayerfully submitted to God for His approval and possible modification, this clarity can make our life more significant and productive. For we will be doing not simply what is expected of us, but what is creatively new.

Eyes to See:

Finding What Is Close at Hand

Answers to our many questions and healing for our hurts do not always lie far away. They are frequently close at hand. Our difficulty is that sometimes we look in the wrong places. At other times we are too fretful or preoccupied to see. But sometimes we fail to see because we cannot possibly believe that God would be kind enough to care about us, to provide us with answers, to give us hope, and to gently renew us.

Nouwen addresses God in this way: "You are so close to me if I am but willing to open the eyes you have given me."[35] We thus need eyes to see. And seeing eyes are eyes of faith. Eyes that look beyond the problem. Eyes that look beyond our own unworthiness. Eyes that look with confidence to the God of all grace and mercy.

When we care to look in this way, we will often find that some answers already lie close at hand. That the seeds of hope are already present. That some steps can be taken that head us in the right direction. Sometimes we may discover that God has already acted on our behalf. That there is an open door. That there is a way we can take. Our problem was that we simply failed to see what was already there, for we were too consumed by our difficulties.

Conversations of the Heart:

Developing the Prayer of Openness

In prayer, not only the mind but also the heart must speak. Our true feelings must be expressed. Our heartfelt questions must be leveled at our Creator. Our doubts must be brought out in the open. Our disappointments and our concerns must be spoken.

Prayer has nothing to do with politeness. It is not simply a fireside chat. It is often the cry of the heart. It is the speech of passion. It is the occasion where our doubts and hopes, our fear and faith mingle together as we pour out what bothers us and what we long for. The speech of the heart is not always quiet, affirming, and nurturing. Nor is it always full of faith and charity. It is sometimes full of anguish. It may even be irrational and incoherent.

But it cries for answers. It looks for relief. It is born of hope and not of anger. It is born of pain and not of bitterness. It springs from a relationship that is strong enough to deal with the hard and the real issues, and it does not need to hide anything because it fears rejection. Nouwen rightly points out that "prayer heals. Not just the answer to prayer."[36]

But it is not any and every prayer that heals. It is the prayer of the heart, the prayer of openness, the prayer that cries out to the Lord that brings relief, peace, and healing.

The Gift of Hospitality:

Creating Space for the Guest

One of the most significant ways to serve others is to be present to them. Present not in a smothering or controlling way, but in providing a place of freedom. Such a place can be provided through the ministry of hospitality.

Nouwen points out that hospitality means "the creation of a free space where the stranger can enter and become a friend."[37] Hospitality is thus a gift that we can give to the other person.

Hospitality does not necessarily mean doing something special for the guest or friend. It means being ourselves and allowing another into the rhythm of our family or community life. It means sharing a meal, providing a room. But more importantly, it means being willing both to share something of ourselves and of our life journey and being open to participate in those things that the guest or friend may share.

But hospitality is not only about sharing. It is also providing a free space, providing room where the guest can be still and at peace. Hospitality is not entertainment. It is not crowding the guest. It is a rhythm that allows for freedom and participation in which the guest can be enriched. In exercising such a ministry, we ourselves will also be enriched.

Our Responsibility:

Being Both Mystic and Activist

The mystic and the activist are not two different ways of being in the world, with the one committed to withdrawal and the other to participation. These two ways ought to be complementary. Activism should drive us to reflection and inner renewal. And the search for prayerful solitude should motivate us to embrace the concerns of the world.

The danger for the mystic is escapism. The danger for the activist is burnout and a gradual loss of perspective.

In suggesting that the two belong together, we wish to see the activist embrace a life of prayer and the mystic embrace a costly worldly concern. Seeking to be both signals our growth in responsibility. Nouwen points out that it is "only through facing up to the reality of our world that we can grow into our own responsibility."[38] At the same time, it is only through facing up to the reality of our own needs, lack of resources, pain, weakness, and limitation that we grow into responsibility for others and for their growth and development.

Growth in responsibility is never only growth in concern for others while negating our own needs. Growth in responsibility is never only growth for ourselves while denying the call to serve others, the cry of the poor, the alienation of our neighbor, and the commitment to a solidarity with our brothers and sisters in the faith.

Companionship:

Doing Things Together

We often think that service is doing things *for* others. That sometimes needs to be. But service takes on its true character when we do things *with* others. This is never an easy road to travel. It is the slow road requiring much patience and care. It gives credit to what another may contribute. It takes on the pace of another.

We find it easier to do things for others. We can then be our quick and efficient selves. We can then set the terms and conditions. We can then be available or withdraw when it suits us. Such service may make us feel good, but it frequently disempowers the other person.

Nouwen, from his experience of working with mentally and physically disabled persons at L'Arche, came to realize that true service "asks for a deep inner conviction that a slow job done together is better than a fast job done alone."[39] Such service does not have a quick end result in view. It has a process in view. It sees service as a joining with the other. It sees service as a companionship and walking a common road for a period of time.

As We Are:

Responding to the Other's Accepting Love

We can take our disappointments, failures, and mistakes too seriously. We do this when we decide to hold onto them or do nothing about them. More seriously, we can take our mistakes to be an essential description of our person. Thus we label ourselves as a failure, a victim, or a wrongdoer. In making these moves, we not only lock ourselves into certain descriptions, but we produce self-fulfilling prophecies. We become what we think we are.

The short circuit to this spiral is not to try valiantly to avoid making mistakes. Perfectionism is not the answer to despair.

Instead, we need to learn to come with our disappointments, failures, and mistakes to a place of acknowledgment and unburdening. Nouwen gently reminds us that "God does not require a pure heart before embracing us."[40] We are loved with our disappointments and failures. We are invited in spite of our wrongdoing. We can come home even though we have wandered. We can start again even though things have gone all wrong. We do not need to stay where we are.

The secret of the spiritual life is not to achieve a state of bliss while having become blind to our mistakes. Instead, the secret is to recognize that the Great Lover welcomes us as we are—not to pity us, but to gently transform us and inspire us with new hope.

Gentle Moves:

Ways to Spiritual Growth

We can be too soft on ourselves and make excuses for our wrongdoing and sins. But we can also be too hard on ourselves. We can expect too much of ourselves, especially regarding our spiritual growth and development. We somehow think that our spiritual growth should follow with our experience of other aspects of life. There we can see definite signs of progress that are clearly measurable. We complete courses, projects, work assignments. We are given more responsibility and receive greater remuneration. We can clearly track the development of our careers.

But we cannot do quite the same with the spiritual life. One reason is that much of that life is hidden deeply within us. Some of it remains a mystery. Most of it cannot be quantified. And the rules are so very different from the way we experience things at work.

For in the spiritual life, progress sometimes means going back. Maturity involves childlikeness. Having means letting go. We can safely say that the spiritual life operates on a different wisdom, and all the pushing and shoving that so characterizes our workaday world will hardly serve us in our spiritual growth. We cannot push our spiritual growth and make it happen with quick-fix methods.

Instead, we need to begin to make gentle moves, moves born of a wisdom from above. In discovering that wisdom, we will learn with Nouwen that "I do not have to move faster than I can."[41] My spiritual development won't result from driven behavior. It will only come from careful listening, quiet surrender, and active and purposeful engagement. It will come from what I do, but only from what is done in harmony with God's wisdom. Most of all, it will come from what was given, not what was expected.

The Prayer of the Heart:

A Way of Perservering

We have noticed that solitude is not a place. It is, more particularly, a state of being. But this state of being needs to be maintained. Inner peace and resolve can easily become dissipated.

Similarly, prayer is not simply attending the place of prayer. Prayer is not simply maintaining a certain discipline where we tell God all that we desire or need. Prayer can also be a state of being. This is the prayer of the heart. This is the prayer that Nouwen tells us "continues to pray within me."[42] This is a prayer that becomes a part of me. The prayer that I cannot continue to live without. It is the prayer that reverberates within my being. It is a prayer that grows within me, just like a baby within a mother's womb, and that knows no rest until it has come to resolution.

The prayer of the heart is sometimes as basic as "Please God, don't let me go." Sometimes it is hunger to know God more fully and His ways more truly. At other times, the prayer of the heart is an intercessory prayer where we consistently carry someone with needs in our heart.

While the prayer of the heart can take on many forms and may center on particular concerns, its abiding characteristic is that it is with us whether we pray, work, eat, or sleep. It is a prayer that is maintained not by an act of the will, but by our very being.

Keeping the Flame Alive:

Guarding the Inner Life

We sometimes mistakenly think that every thought should be expressed, every vision proclaimed, and every dream explained. We think that everything that takes place in our inner world is ultimately meant for public consumption.

This is clearly not the case. There are things that are sacred and private. We don't usually divulge the intimacies of our love life to others. Similarly, there are intimacies of our interior being that should remain hidden. Nouwen notes that "silence is the discipline by which the inner fire of God is tended and kept alive."[43] It is in the quietness of our own being that thoughts can be carefully nurtured.

It is there that hopes can be persistently sustained. It is there that dreams can be awakened. In the solitude of our inner life, resolutions can be forged and difficult commitments made. There an uncluttered intimacy can flourish. There the self can be renewed and transformed. There love can grow and the sacred can be guarded and protected.

If this interior life is not maintained, we will weaken our inner strength and dissipate our resolve. We will all the more easily run the risk of being swayed by the dominant voices of our time and run the danger of losing ourselves. To keep what is sacred is not selfishness. It is right to maintain what guards the self. It is, moreover, the seedbed from which courageous actions can flow.

"Poor in Spirit" Silence:

Moving from the Good to the Best

Not any and every silence is productive for coming to solitude. All quietness does not lead to inner peace. Nouwen says: "It is [in] the silence of the 'poor in spirit' where you learn to see life in its proper perspective."[44] This silence is the product of an inner disposition characterized by abandonment and hope.

To be "poor in spirit" is not to be poor-spirited—that is, passive and without drive and initiative. Quite the opposite. It is to be full of spirit—full of plans, desires, and ideas. But also full of the knowledge that everything we plan and desire should not necessarily be carried out; that everything we desire does not always have productive outcomes—and that, therefore, we need to learn the art of abandonment by subjecting our plans and desires to the scrutiny of God's wisdom.

In doing this, we become the candidates for hope. For God's wisdom will open up new possibilities. In laying something aside, fresh perspectives can be gained. And in acknowledging that we don't have all the answers, insight can come from the most unexpected sources.

The silence of the "poor in spirit" is productive in helping us to move from the good to the best, from the spontaneous to the wise, from the impulsive to the most constructive. In this silence we learn to bring ourselves, with all our plans and ideas, to the point of inner surrender and quietude—not in order to be nothing or to do nothing, but in order to know more truly and to act more creatively.

The Challenge of a Friend:

Encouragement in the Journey

The rhythm of the inner life is the movement from where we are, with our fears, needs, and busyness, to the place of quietness, unburdening, and renewal. And from this place of transformation, we can begin to move to reengage our world with newfound hope and courage.

While the practice of this rhythm is a highly personal and individual affair, others can assist us in this journey. While we need to take responsibility for our own spiritual development and for our own lives, this does not mean that we need to be without companions on the road. Nouwen admits: "I now realise that I need regular contact with a friend who keeps me close to Jesus and continues to call me to faithfulness."[45]

Such a friend cannot do the journeying for us. Such a friend cannot provide ready-made answers. Such a friend cannot take away the struggle and cannot take away the pain or difficulty.

There is a road that we alone must walk. Decisions that we must make. Actions that we must perform. Pain that we must bear. Transformation that we must experience. Peace that we must imbibe. But a friend who journeys with us can challenge us to faithfulness and authenticity. Such a friend can assist to keep us honest. Such a friend can encourage us to continue to make the hard decisions. The challenge such a friend offers is the challenge to continue to choose life.

The Risk of Living:

Moving Beyond Safety and Security

We can create a very safe world for ourselves. We establish our work routines. Cultivate a few friendships. Develop certain family patterns. Establish our ideas about God and the meaning of life. Maintain certain spiritual disciplines and take on certain commitments. None of these things in itself need necessarily be inappropriate.

But all this may spring from the doubtful motivation of trying to make for ourselves a safe and secure world. A world that guards us from risks. A world that shelters us from new challenges. A world where the very fabric of our routines not only sustains us, but also anesthetizes us.

The inner life cannot fully develop under these circumstances. Safety is not always a key to growth. But questioning, searching, and risk-taking are. Nouwen makes the observation that the questions we raise "have to be lived rather than developed intellectually."[46] In other words, we need to cease taking our world for granted and begin taking our questions into the arena of life by living them out practically. True questioning can only lead to a new doing. Searching can only lead to shattering some of our securities. And risk-taking, when born of a desire to live more truly and authentically, can only lead to new life.

Grasping the Essential:

Overcoming the Tyranny of the Urgent

Spirituality is not simply an inward disposition. It is not only a peaceful and tranquil state of mind. Spirituality must also come to expression in acts of kindness, deeds of love, and thankful service. Such service need not always be hard, sacrificial, demanding, and burdensome. Service can also be joyful and liberating. It can be an important expression of who we are, an outworking of our gifted-ness, and the realization of impulses that seek to bring about the good and the beautiful.

But service needs to be focused. We cannot do everything. Nouwen makes the realistic observation, "If I were to let my life be taken over by what is urgent, I might very well never get around to what is essential."[47] So often service is the response to the urgent. At times it may well need to be, for we cannot turn away from what needs to be done now.

But service needs to be more than that. It should also have long-term goals in view. It should respond to crisis, but also build for the future. It should respond to need, but also seek to develop structures that may eliminate such need.

In order to serve like this, we need to learn to grasp the essential. And to grasp the essential, we need to be inspired by a vision. We need to have heard the call. We need to be captivated by a sense that "this is what I must do." Such service, no matter how long and arduous the journey on which it may take us, will always be sustained by hope.

Charity, the Purpose of the Inner Life:

Maintaining Our Focus

We can easily fall into the trap of forgetting the reasons why we do certain things. And so we begin to lose our way.

We embark, for example, on a particular direction and put certain strategies in place, but become so caught up in the doing and the maintaining of those strategies that we begin to forget what we were seeking to achieve in the first place. In other words, it is easy for us to become diverted. It is easy to forget our goals and objectives.

This is also true in the exercise of the disciplines of the inner life. The desire to be still may spring out of the need to reevaluate our life and its direction. But once we have tasted the initial fruit of our quest and have gained some new insight, we easily become distracted. We thus fail to press for deeper changes. And the discipline to be still takes on all other kinds of dimensions. In fact, we can become preoccupied with stillness for stillness' sake.

Nouwen reminds us that "charity, not stillness, is the purpose of the spiritual life."[48] This is not to suggest that the exercise of the discipline of stillness should not serve to help us to reevaluate, gain new strength for the journey, deepen our self-understanding, give new depth to our prayers, and deepen our intimacy with the Great Lover who calls us to new life. The disciplines of the inner life can serve these and many other purposes.

But in the final analysis, they are not there to be utilized simply for ourselves. They are to be utilized in order that we may love and serve more generously and purposefully. If we forget to maintain this important purpose, the fruit that springs from our inner life will be unripe. It will not only be tasteless for others, but it will have a sour and bitter taste in our own mouths.

Overpowered:

Regaining Control over Our Life's Direction

We would like to think that we are always in control of our own lives and that we have the power to make purposeful decisions. Sadly, this is not always the case. We are not always in control. Sometimes our circumstances seem to rule our lives much more than our own decisions. Sometimes the consequences of previous unfortunate decisions plague us in the present. And frequently the demands of the present and pressures of the moment dominate our lives. We can feel overpowered. We feel overwhelmed and frequently begin to slide into resentment or fantasizing.

One move that we can begin to make as an alternative to these negative options is to create a place of stillness where we face the "enemies" who are ranged against us. Nouwen notes that "when you are able to create a lonely place in the middle of your actions and concerns, your successes and failures slowly can lose some of their power over you."[49] So the pressure of the moment, the demands of others, the expectations of loved ones, the unresolved issues of the past, and the power of our own compulsions can lose some of their hold over our lives.

In the place of stillness, quiet reflection, and ruthless honesty, we can begin to reclaim the ground that has been lost. We can take a stand and retake the reins of our lives.

We do this not by willing that things be different. Nor by fretful prayer. Nor by plotting plans to escape. We regain lost territory by rediscovering that we are more than the work of our own hands. That we are loved for who we are by the God of all compassion, not merely for what we do. And, by creating space for ourselves, we can gain a new perspective on the pressures and the demands that we experience and so can begin to plot a new course for our lives.

Finding Peace Within:

Learning to Be at Home with Ourselves

We need to come to an inner peace if our life is to be perennially productive. Such inner peace is a fruit of the way we consistently live. It is not the product of an escape from our circumstances — although we frequently think that a change of circumstances will provide us with the answers we seek and the peace we long for.

Peace comes from being at home with ourselves. It comes from being thankful for the way God has made and gifted us. It comes from the joy of giving and an appreciation for all we receive. It comes from accepting ourselves and celebrating all that is good, while working on what needs to change.

Peace comes from being loved and having the satisfaction of achievement and the challenge of new goals. Peace wells up from within, but it is clearly related to the way we live and the choices we make.

But it is seldom the result of much-having. It does not necessarily come with great success. Instead, it is the unexpected gift. It is the surprise. It is there even when we didn't expect it. It remains even when the going is tough. And it can grow in the midst of pain and difficulty.

If peace finds its expression in being at home with ourselves, we clearly need to stop looking elsewhere. Nouwen laments the fact that "we do not trust our innermost self as an intimate place." He notes that we "anxiously wander around hoping to find [peace] where we are not."[50] Because peace is not simply the fruit of our circumstances, it can only come from within. And it can only abide there if we are at peace with ourselves.

The Heart of Our Existence:

The Nature of True Spirituality

We are far more secular, pragmatic, rationalistic, and achievement-oriented than we would like to think. We are frequently "the children of this age." We have absorbed far more of the values of this age than we have recognized. We strive for similar goals. Set similar priorities. Hold similar ideals. And frequently live out similar values.

This is so because we have not taken sufficient heed of Nouwen's dictum that "the spiritual life has to do with the heart of existence."[51] The attention we give to the spiritual life is frequently marginal. It is concerned with special religious activities, but not with lifestyle. It is concerned with worship, but not with values. Its focus is blessing, but not commitment. Its concern is prayer, but not service.

The spiritual life, however, has nothing to do with touching the edges of our lives. Its value does not lie in transforming the periphery of who we are. Its purpose is not simply to add some extra qualities to our lives. The spiritual life has to do with the very core of our existence. The inner life is not a quiet inner sanctuary that remains segregated from the more central and mundane aspects of our lives. The spiritual life is transformative. It challenges us at the very center of our being and seeks to permeate every facet of our existence.

It is strange that we give this dynamism so little attention. It is frequently seen as the luxury of the few, rather than the passion of the many. It is seen as the preoccupation of the few, rather than the norm for the many. Yet those who give the development of the inner life its true priority will not be found wanting in virtue, strength, vision, and purpose.

The Matter of Balance:

Growing into Wholeness

We frequently play one priority, discipline, or grace against another. We emphasize one thing only to neglect another. For example, we pray, but fail to work. We serve, but fail to be inwardly renewed. To hold together various spiritual disciplines, priorities, and emphases remains one of our biggest challenges—and one of our most pressing needs.

We soon discover that balance and harmony are not easily achieved. We are so often one-sided. We enthusiastically grasp at particular strategies and methods, only to discard them again. And in the meantime we have neglected disciplines that were at least moderately useful.

We therefore need to recognize that balance and harmony need to be wrested from our ever-present tendency to find singular solutions and easy answers. They need to be won from our habitual tendency to make the part the whole and to major on minors. To bring things into balance and harmony in our lives, however, will never finally depend on methods. This can only spring from a wisdom forged in experience.

Nouwen reminds us that the "balance between silence and words, withdrawal and involvement, distance and closeness, solitude and community"[52] forms the basis of the spiritual life. To this we may add giving and receiving, holding and relinquishing, suffering and healing, prayer and work, and the sacred and the secular—these all form part of the mosaic of the inner life. It is when these seeming opposites all blend together to operate in our lives that the quest for balance has begun.

All Our Concerns:

The Practice of Prayer

The one who prays is not someone who is engaged in a flight from reality. Prayer is not escapism. It is not self-negation. It is not wanting something magical to happen. It is not saying, "I am helpless and hopeless and therefore I need God's help." Prayer is nothing like that at all. It is quite the opposite.

Prayer is self-assertion, not self-abnegation. It is saying, "I need to live fully and purposefully and, therefore, I need wisdom, direction, and encouragement from a source beyond myself." Prayer faces the real world; it is not world-denying.

Nouwen reminds us that the "characteristic of the prayer of the heart is that it includes all our concerns."[53] The true practice of prayer brings our whole world and all our struggles and issues into dialogue with the One who persistently loves us.

Prayer seeks for wisdom, not simply answers. It looks for courage, not simply help. It seeks for the gift of persistence, not simply quick solutions.

Prayer means being true to ourselves. It involves acknowledging what is really happening to us. But it wisely recognizes that we ourselves don't have all the answers. This has nothing to do with an unhealthy self-negation. It is simply acknowledging our own limitations. And that has everything to do with a healthy realism.

The Outward Call:

*Responding Without Depleting
Our Inner Life*

We are constantly called outward. There is so
much to do. So many things demand our attention—children, house duties, work, and friendships.
Even our recreation and rest are often taken up with
outward responses. Room and time for inwardness are
hard to create and to find in our busy world. Nouwen
laments that "to reach the inner sanctum where God's
voice and direction can be heard and obeyed is not easy
if you are always called outward."[54]

The outward momentum not only occurs when
we are busy doing things. This is often only a small
part of it. The major part is the thinking and planning,
the worrying and fretting, and the restless drivenness
of our inner life.

Thus it is not only that we are busy doing things,
nor that we spend a lot of time thinking about what
should be done; it is also that we become restless when
there is nothing on our immediate horizon. We are
therefore outwardly focused even when we have the
opportunity to enter the inner sanctuary for refreshment and renewal.

The challenge, therefore, is not only to learn to
pace ourselves, to set limits, and to say no. It is not
simply a matter of learning to do less so that we have
more time for ourselves. It is also a matter of creatively
using time for ourselves. While such time should

involve relaxation, it should more importantly involve inner renewal, for we deplete our inner resources much more quickly than we realize. Equally importantly, it should also involve gaining new directions and insights, lest we constantly make the same mistakes and fail to establish patterns that facilitate growth.

In Everyday Life:

A Spirituality of Daily Life

Religious behavior is sometimes an escape from the real world. This can express itself in a pining for the world to come or in expecting quick solutions to pressing problems that don't involve our participation in the answer.

This can also express itself in a pietism that separates one from other people or in an asceticism that negates normal life experiences. Such religious attitudes, while they may be appealing to some because they define spirituality in easily identifiable behavior, help little in our quest for holism.

Spirituality has nothing to do with escapism. It has everything to do with facing the real world. Nouwen suggests that a true spirituality should "reveal the first lines of the new world behind the veil of everyday life."[55] To express that somewhat differently, ordinary life can be impregnated with the sacred. The ordinary can be imbued with spiritual meaning. In fact, it cannot be any other way.

For it is in our everyday life that we must find purpose and direction. It is in our everyday life that we need to experience growth, development, well-being, and challenge. It is in our everyday life that we need to express our faith. And it is in our everyday life that we need to experience that God is with us.

We therefore cannot experience God's grace only in the sanctuary. This must also be experienced in everyday life. God's presence cannot be experienced only at the place of prayer. In daily life we also need to know God's participation and sustenance.

Thus we need to fully participate in this life. But we don't live only for this life. We also have a future hope. And in this life we can catch glimpses of what that future hope may look like.

Built on Deeds:

Building Community Through Loving Service

Community is not built by wishful thinking. It is not achieved by dreaming. It does not come about simply by longing for a place of friendship, meaningful relationships, and solidarity. Neither is community achieved only by prayer.

Community, that fragile gift of commonality, is built on deeds. It comes about when people are prepared to love and serve each other. It emerges when we are prepared to find meaningful common goals and purposes. It grows when we can continue to find sufficient reasons to journey together. And it becomes rich when it encourages diversity within unity.

Nouwen reminds us that a community such as L'Arche, which comprises intellectually and physically handicapped persons, "is built not on words, but on a body." With this observation he wishes to emphasize the practicality of being in community with those who cannot fully care for themselves. From this experience Nouwen makes the observation that "feeding, cleaning, touching, holding—this is what builds the community."[56]

This observation, however, holds true for any community. We cannot have a life together unless it comes to expression through practical care and service. And it cannot be sustained unless we respond to the call to lay aside our pride, priorities, and position and clothe ourselves with the garment of humility.

The secret of community lies not in its creative and enthusiastic genesis. It lies not in its great moments of celebration and revelation. Rather, it lies in the daily rhythm of faithful and joyful service.

Touching the Lowly Places:

The Ministry of Care

Seeking to be helpful to another person is never easy. It may be fraught with difficulties and fears. We are frequently unsure whether we can be really helpful or whether the person really wants our help. We are also uncertain as to what might be most helpful and beneficial. And we never fully understand all that may be involved in a person's needs and struggles.

Yet we need to be careful that we don't make it all so complicated that we are paralyzed into inactivity. This is not to say that we should rush in with our good intentions, which might be wide of the mark. Careful listening and sensitivity are always called for. But the important thing is that we start where we can and respond to what is at hand.

This simple start might possibly lead to new opportunities and further ways to serve the other person. It takes time to build bridges of trust and openness. This is so even for people who are pressed by deep needs. It therefore takes time to come to the place where we can serve another more meaningfully.

Nouwen notes that we need "to bend ourselves to the ground and touch the places in each other that most need washing."[57] This suggests carefulness, humility, and trust. It involves a joining together. But it also involves a mutuality. Once we move beyond the crises and continue to serve, we ourselves will also receive. Those to whom we give will also enrich us.

Learning to Trust:

The Art of Trusting Your Own Discernment

As adults we don't easily and readily come to the point of trusting someone else. In this we are so unlike children. Growth in trust for us is a long and tenuous journey. It usually requires a lot of reassurances along the way.

Learning to trust is not only difficult because we are unsure of the other person. It is all the more difficult because we are unsure of ourselves. We often don't know what we are really expecting from and wanting of the other person. And because we are driven by our own fears and insecurities, we frequently undermine the credibility of the other person. Or more seriously, we discredit the good he or she does and fail to give the trust that is his or her due.

Learning to trust is thus a risk-taking venture. We need to risk our own fears by seeking to overcome them and risk our uncertainty of the other by welcoming that person. Learning to trust others is one thing; learning to trust ourselves is another. But learning to trust God is intimately related to both. We can hardly trust God regarding His care and love for us if we cannot trust others who seek to be instruments of that care and love. And we can hardly trust God's purpose and direction for our lives if we are constantly racked by self-doubt.

Learning to trust is thus not just an "other people" problem. The issue is not simply whether others can be trusted. It is more importantly a question of whether I can be at peace within myself so that

I can be open to others; whether I can trust my own discernment; whether I can help to build bridges of relationship and understanding; and whether I am loved enough to be loving.

Nouwen recognizes that learning to trust is frequently our problem and our struggle. He acknowledges the problem in this prayer: "I trust in you, Lord, but keep helping me in my many moments of distrust and doubt."[58]

The Matter of Anger:

Learning to Face the Issues at Hand

We invariably find it hard to start with ourselves. This may sound surprising when we live in a society so characterized by self-interest. Yet it is true that we find it difficult to take a good, hard look at ourselves first, particularly when it comes to reevaluation and problem-solving.

Problems, in our estimation, tend to lie with the other person, and answers have to come from somewhere "out there." Some forms of spirituality have wrongly encouraged this approach. In its most deformed and simplistic form, this operates on the idea that answers must come from God and problems are from the Devil.

Sadly, this approach totally bypasses our responsibility and our participation. Wrongdoing always involves our participation, even when we wish to claim that we were unwittingly seduced. And answers involve our seeking, searching, and questioning, as well as our digesting, embracing, and acting. Thus, both in creating the difficulties and in finding the solutions, we play our part. And because we play a part, we have a lot to do with the persons we are becoming. It is not simply external forces that create our difficulties and shape our lives. We ourselves also create the tone and tenor of our lives. We do so by facing life realistically, by making good choices, and by seeking to live with integrity.

Important in the shaping of our lives is learning

to deal with the issues at hand. Our present anger, for example, when that has been destructive, should be addressed now—particularly because we are able to look at its genesis, shape, and outworking.

If we persistently put it off and blame others or expect magical answers, wrong anger will become a shadowy reality that will etch an unfortunate pattern into the fabric of our being. Nouwen, in speaking of an "anger which settles into a biting resentment and slowly paralyses a generous heart,"[59] signals for us a gradual but significant degeneration.

We therefore need to learn to come sooner rather than later to the scene of our own actions in order to put things right. Delay only reinforces our lack of responsibility. Learning to face the issues at hand, particularly our own issues, will free us for creative problem-solving in which we may play a part, but in which we can also experience the grace, healing, and forgiveness of the God who always calls us to the light.

Hindrances Become a Way:

The Creative Use of Difficulty

Creating space for ourselves, learning to be still, and entering into solitude serve not only our spiritual development. These disciplines also help us to become our own persons. It is a way in which we can become sure of who we are, what we believe, and what we must do. Solitude is a way of self-formation.

Solitude is also a way of making us more resourceful and creative. It can help us to reorient our thinking so that, in the words of Nouwen, "what seems a hindrance becomes a way."[60] This is not easy. Hindrances and difficulties often frustrate us. They can make us angry at others, and even at God. They make us feel victimized and can drive us to self-doubt and despair. We prefer to sidestep difficulties. We feel that we have run out of luck when too many hindrances stare us in the face. We curse fate and we doubt God's benevolence and care. We seldom do well in difficulty.

This is often due to the fact that we lack inner resources and a strong resolve. We see hindrances and difficulties as "just one more thing on our plate" that we don't have time for.

And yet we could learn so much if we faced our difficulties. Sometimes difficulties can tell us much about ourselves. They can always tell us something about our world. And they can usually teach us something regarding new ways of responding and acting.

It is difficulty that has inspired some members of the human race to great creativity. Difficulty is an important factor in change. It is also the way in which we can become more careful and prayerful. And sometimes, when we take the time to be still and face the difficulties before us, we discover that they were not what they at first seemed—a hindrance—but were in fact a way to new experiences.

Loneliness as a Gift:

Preserving Our Separateness

The very thing that we may wish to overcome or wish would go away can often be the source of growth and renewal. The reason for this is that often we don't know what is best for us. Moreover, we are preoccupied with eating the fruit and fail to give adequate attention to the root from which good things grow.

Nouwen reminds us, in this regard, that a growth-promoting "way of life does not take away our loneliness; it protects and cherishes it as a precious gift."[61] We, however, see loneliness as a problem. We don't see it as a root from which good things can spring. We simply feel the emotional pain of being alone.

We undermine our sense of self-worth as a result of it. And so we throw ourselves into relationships, merge into the crowd, demand to be loved, compulsively form friendships, fill our agendas, and crowd our own space only to discover that we need to be alone. Sadly, we often discover what we really need only after we have become satiated with its opposite.

Loneliness, therefore, need not be a reflection on our self-worth. It is rather the place where we can discover our true self. It is a place of sanctity. It is a gift that ought to be cherished, for it not only separates us "far from the madding crowd," but it also helps us to find that inner security from which we can make our friendships, build our relationships, and engage in life's pursuits without that compulsive drive that finally destroys rather than builds.

The Quiet Center:

The Place of Humility

We have been stressing that life without self-reflection leads to our losing our way. In the words of Nouwen, "A life without a lonely place, that is, without a quiet centre, easily becomes destructive."[62]

As we have seen, the quiet place not only helps us to develop a sense of our own separateness and identity; it also helps us to identify and to deal with the issues that cause us pain and sadness. There we can resolve to deal with our anger and discover creative ways to deal with difficulty.

But the quiet place is not simply the place where we overcome difficulties. It is also the place where we can gain new inspiration and direction.

We need to realize, however, that the quiet place itself cannot produce these good things. More importantly, we ourselves cannot produce these good things. The quiet place is not the place of cleverness where we sort ourselves out and come up with marvelous answers.

The quiet place is not where we exult in the self. It is a very different place. It is the place of humility. The place of prayer. The place where we realize our limitations. It is the place where we ask questions of ourselves. Where we ask the Holy Spirit to reveal things to us. Where we learn to listen to our frequently suppressed inner voice. Where our conscience is listened to. Where our sense of fair play and justice gains priority. Where forgiveness predominates. And where creative solutions and answers emerge through inspiration and revelation.

The quiet place is thus ultimately the place where we receive what comes as a surprise and a gift. This can only affirm to us that we are blessed rather than smart and self-sufficient.

Silence:

The Place for Building Relationships

At first glance, silence as a place for building relationships sounds like a contradiction in terms.

Surely the search for silence is to get away from
people? Surely it has to do with getting away from our
busy world with all its demands? This is only partly
true. One can also experience solitude in the midst of
daily life. As such, it is an inner disposition of peace
and tranquility, of prayer and quiet reflection that we
maintain despite the hustle and bustle of life.

But even when we withdraw to a quiet place, does
this mean that we are really withdrawing? In fact the opposite can be the case. We can withdraw out of concern for
others. We can be so concerned about connecting with
people, wanting to deepen our friendships or desiring to
build new relationships with a stranger, neighbor, or
coworker, that we seek the quiet place in order to reflect
and pray. We do so in order to find a wisdom and a love
that will facilitate our relationship-building. Nouwen
speaks of people entering into "that silence in which they
can discover themselves, each other and God."[63]

We don't enter into solitude just to find ourselves.
The place of silence sometimes needs to be crowded with
others. Those others are the objects of our concern and
love. In the quiet place we think of them. We pray for
them. We bless them. We wish them well. And we think
of ways by which we can encourage, help, challenge, and
serve them when we meet.

Thus the place of silence is not only the place
where we are alone. It is also the place to which we
bring those others who are the concern of our hearts.

The Wounded Healer:

Serving in Spite of Our Own Struggles

It is clearly not true that we have to be perfect before we can help another person. This is so not only in the realm of the practical, but also in the spiritual. Ministry does not only flow from strength; it also comes from weakness.

It is also not true that we can only help another to the extent that we ourselves have been helped. It is not even true that we cannot "grow" another person beyond the point to which we ourselves have grown.

Frequently a "wounded healer" is used to bring hope and well-being to another, which results in growth well beyond that experienced by the giver. Sometimes the wounded healer can bring to the other the very blessing and healing for which the healer himself or herself is seeking.

Nouwen reminds us that frequently one "must look after his own wounds, but at the same time be prepared to heal the wounds of others."[64] There is nothing inappropriate about this—as if one should be so ashamed of one's own "wounds" that one is paralyzed into inactivity. In fact, there is something quite wonderful about this seeming paradox. How wonderful that our own difficulties need not prevent us from doing good, that in spite of our own pain, we can still bring encouragement to others!

The wounded healer is not the exception to the rule. When helpers are honest with themselves, they will readily acknowledge that they, too, have needs. These needs are not necessarily a handicap. In fact, they can make us deeply understanding and aware of the struggles of others.

Mobilizing Our Pain:

The Move from Difficulty to Hope

Suffering, difficulty, and disappointment are our common lot. We are unrealistic if we think that these only befall the "unfortunate." Suffering befalls poor and rich, the fortunate and the unfortunate, even though the form of suffering and difficulty will undoubtedly be different for these varying groups of people.

Some difficulties are clearly of our own making. For these we need to assume personal responsibility by working toward their resolution. Other difficulties come our way, beyond our own willing and doing. For these we may not always be able to take some corrective action.

But we do need to respond to these difficulties with creativity and courage lest they overwhelm us and embitter our lives. The challenge is to mobilize our pain and not to waste our sorrows. Nouwen speaks of the need to mobilize our pains into a common search for life so that these "very pains are transformed from expressions of despair into signs of hope."[65]

While pain and difficulty may be our common lot, we are not to accept passively this state of affairs. Pain and difficulty need to become transformed. And while that transformation may not always result in the hoped-for solutions, it can always result in a greater hope and faith. A hope that continues to choose life. A hope that actively resists evil. A hope that sees beyond the personal and carries the birth pangs of the new order. And a hope that sustains us in a faithfulness in the face of difficulty.

Maturity and Childlikeness:

Rhythms of the Spiritual Journey

Our spiritual life does not follow the pattern of our physical and social development. Physically and emotionally we grow from childhood into adulthood. And unless we are psychologically or socially underdeveloped, we leave that childhood phase behind us.

It is not quite like that with our spiritual growth. We are encouraged to grow from "babes in Christ" into spiritual maturity. But spiritual maturity does not necessarily mean strength, competence, and independence. It does not mean that we have arrived.

Maturity also involves openness and further learning. More importantly, in our spiritual journey we often have to learn old lessons again. Moral issues that we thought we had under control resurface. Intellectual questions that we thought we had squared away come to plague us once again. Issues of commitment and obedience that we assumed were firmly in place shake themselves loose with changing circumstances. And matters of faithfulness, truthfulness, and integrity ever call into question so much of what we do. It is these realities that bring home to us the call to be childlike.

This certainly does not mean that we should be childish and immature. Instead, it means that we should be open, not so sure of ourselves, trusting in God to help us, ready to learn more, and willing to be led by God's hand.

Sadly for some, added years have produced a hardness and an attitude of "I know it all." Maturity has, for others, become synonymous with self-confidence and independence.

The call to be childlike calls that into question. Not only do we need to acknowledge what others contribute to our lives, but we also need to thank God for the sustaining work of His Spirit in our lives. We thus move from strength to weakness, maturity to child-likeness, and giving to receiving and back again in the rhythm of our spiritual life.

Nouwen notes, "I am very weak and fragile precisely where I thought I had the most to give."[66] In this he not only reminds us that we may not always be as strong and mature as we think, but he also implies that sometimes our apparent weakness can be our strength. Similarly, childlikeness can be a powerful attitude in our ongoing development.

Discovering the "Unadorned Self":

Running the Risk of Losing Power

We can stop growing. We can stop developing into the persons we could potentially be. We can foreclose on this process by clinging to what we have and to what we know and by elevating security over risk-taking. Or we can continue to be called forward.

One powerful way to be called forward is to discover what Nouwen calls the "unadorned self." This he describes as a state "in which I am completely vulnerable, open to receive and give love regardless of any accomplishments."[67]

This discovery can hardly occur while we maintain our regular priorities and are surrounded by our familiar world. This discovery will seldom occur while our world is secure and we revel with satisfaction in all that we have built, produced, and accomplished.

Nouwen's discovery of the "unadorned self" occurred in the challenging but painful transition from teaching at the prestigious Harvard and Yale universities to his involvement in one of the L'Arche communities for intellectually and physically disabled persons. There the former accomplishments meant nothing, and previous achievements were more of a disadvantage than an asset.

Discovering the "unadorned self" can occur in all our places of transition: the move from singleness to marriage, health to sickness, religious life to secular employment, privilege to voluntary relinquishment, power to abandonment, security to risk-taking, youth to adulthood, satisfaction to searching, certainty to questioning, and faith to seeking.

Discovering the unadorned or vulnerable self may well feel like a depowering experience. But in our openness to maximize on the potentiality of our new circumstances or our new state of being, we can become empowered with a new and richer self.

Prayer Friend:

Nourishing the Inner Life

It is a paradox that in this time in history when we have created the megalopolis and therefore live in increasingly crowded spaces, we can experience so much loneliness. It is a further paradox that, in spite of the major advances in medical technology, we are still so unwell and that, in spite of the communication revolution, we still feel so alienated. We can safely say that whatever we seem to create at a societal level, however good it is, it also has negative implications.

But more deeply, our difficulties cannot simply be laid at the feet of society. They also lie within us. And at the heart is our lack of a nourishing inner life. We often feel deeply lonely, purposeless, frustrated, misunderstood, and unloved. Our brave front and our many achievements don't ease the pain of our inner poverty.

The enrichment of our inner life is therefore not an optional extra. It is life itself. It will allow us to hold our achievements with open hands in the realization that we are more than our accomplishments. It will also allow us to respond creatively to difficulty because we have wells to draw from that need never be dry.

Prayer is one way of nourishing the inner life. This is so, as Nouwen reminds us, because "the praying man is he who comes out of his shelter and not only has the courage to see his own poverty, but also sees that there is no enemy to hide from, only a friend who would like nothing better than to clothe him with his own coat."[68]

Allowing Ourselves to Be Led:

Prayer and Responsibility

In these reflections we have stressed the importance of personal responsibility. We are not to see ourselves as passive in a difficult world. We don't simply react to what is happening around us. And we don't see ourselves as moved by God without playing a responsible part.

We have stressed that we are called to make choices, take initiatives, run risks, take up challenges, create opportunities, embark on adventures, and at times take steps of faith—the outcomes of which lie well beyond our present knowing.

However, the stress on responsibility is not an argument for self-sufficiency. In fact, the opposite is true. The person who can act responsibly and daringly in our world is a person who is loved and nurtured. Such a person is inwardly replenished. Such a person is open to advice and encouragement. But even more importantly, and possibly surprisingly to some, such a person is a person of prayer.

Unfortunately, we have often played against each other responsibility and prayer. The prayerful person is seen in escapist terms, while the responsible person is seen only in pragmatic terms. This contrast is a false one. Nothing can fuel the actions of our responsibility more than the fragile certainty that God has led us in this direction and that He is calling us to play our part.

Nouwen reminds us that the person "who prays . . . has the courage to stretch out his arms and let himself be led."[69]

Prayer is thus not simply telling God our concerns, but hearing from Him what is on His heart. It is not simply asking Him to help us in the things we are already doing; it is also being led in new directions. It is when we are led by God's Spirit in new directions that our actions of responsibility can enjoy the companionship of the God who journeys with us when we seek to do His will.

Actions and Consequences:

Sowing Good Seed for Good Results

We live in a refractory and difficult world. Our experience confirms this. Things do not always work out, despite our careful planning.

This does not mean, however, that everything is random. Some things do follow. When we freely forgive a person who has hurt us, we can be sure that we will banish bitterness from our hearts. When we serve others, not out of guilt or compulsion, but out of love, we ourselves will be blessed. When we give, not because we expect to receive, but freely and with a generous heart, we will receive. When we become women and men of prayer, we will grow in spiritual wisdom. When we live in obedience to God's will, our lives will be fruitful.

Things, however, follow not only in the spiritual realm, but in the practical as well. If we take time for solitude and renewal, we will be refreshed. If we care for our souls, our bodies will also be blessed.

Nouwen asserts that "he who has the day will gain the night as well."[70] If our day is spent purposefully, the blessing of a good night's rest will be ours as well. Good actions can have good consequences. Good seed can produce good fruit.

Sadly, we often focus too much on results and not enough on the factors that produce such results. We want to pluck fruit from trees we have not planted and watered. We want to be blessed without walking the road of obedience. We want to experience well-being without caring for our own bodies. We want inner peace without being honest and transparent.

Yet we can have what we want. But this will involve sowing and watering. It will involve laying good foundations. It will involve doing what is right ahead of what suits us. It may well involve walking the seemingly long road of faith and obedience rather than taking shortcuts to grasp the promised goal.

The Little Way:

Faithfulness in Our Doing

Every form of good has its shadow. Every blessing has its downside. And every form of strength has its Achilles heel. In understanding the importance of laying good foundations and sowing good seed, we can nevertheless get trapped into always expecting much. And so we live for the promised harvest with its benefits and its abundance and cease to enjoy the present.

The future thus becomes our hope and not the God who has promised to be with us in little and plenty. With this mindset, everything becomes a stepping-stone to something better, and present benefits pale into insignificance. Nouwen admits, "I always want the little way to become the big way."[71]

The issue here is not that we should only expect little. The point is quite different, namely, that there isn't always a direct correlation between what we do by way of preparation and what the outcomes are. Sometimes much preparatory work leads to great results. But sometimes it leads to little. And surprisingly, sometimes the little way does become the big way. But when it does, it should always be a surprise that should lead us to celebration and thankfulness.

The important element in all of this is that our focus should be on faithfully doing what we must, irrespective of whether the outcomes are meager or plentiful.

Servant Leadership:

The Rhythm of Service and Enrichment

The internal pressure and societal constraints on us to be strong, self-sufficient, self-reliant, and independent are enormous. We can easily begin to believe in ourselves so much that we begin to think we are invulnerable. It is easy to believe our own illusions, particularly when they are reinforced by others and held up as achievable ideals by our society.

While being responsible is important, being self-sufficient is an illusion. Leaders particularly feel the pressure to be strong and self-reliant. Not only do they find themselves in situations where they have to operate in this way, but others expect this of them as well. Thus leaders frequently find themselves in positions where they have to continue to give, but are not nourished themselves.

Nouwen calls for a different style of leadership "in which the leader is a vulnerable servant who needs people as much as they need him or her."[72] This form of leadership allows for the rhythm of service and personal enrichment. It means that the leader can be strong as well as admit to times of weakness, struggle, and difficulty. It means that the leader can be giving, but can admit to needing to receive refreshment and encouragement. It, moreover, means that the leader can provide direction, wisdom, and insight, but can also acknowledge uncertainty and limitation.

For this to occur, it will not only necessitate very different attitudes on the part of leaders, but will also

require that those they work with respond very differently. They will have to demystify the role of
leadership and overcome their fears and insecurities.

Where leaders and people link together in the
rhythm of service and enrichment, leaders cannot but
be refreshed and people cannot but grow in responsibility.

Community:

A Way of Service

We cannot be solitary if we are to be growing people. We need others on the pathway of our personal development. Family, friends, a lover, neighbors, and work companions are some of the networks by which we can be enriched.

But networks, or community, are not simply important in our personal formation; they are also the way in which we can contextualize and express our service.

Take counseling, for example. Enjoying a meal in the counselor's home not only helps to contextualize the counselor within her or his family, but also means the person is welcomed as a guest within the family as a small community. Welcoming a person in this way can be as much a source of encouragement as the actual counseling. Sadly, we have disembodied much of the ministry of counseling and relegated it to sterile and impersonal environments.

This model can be extended in many ways. Small communities of care, where those helping and those being served share life together, may well be a more humane place to facilitate growth than in our more traditional institutional models. Nouwen argues for a holistic approach. He notes that we "should not only live in community, but also minister in community."[73]

Such a community, based on mutuality and a common participation, can take on many forms. There is no one model for community. But if we follow Nouwen's suggestion, then we will attempt to bring together that place where we are nurtured and the place of service. In other words, we will not only serve others with our particular helping skills, but also welcome them into our lives.

No Pure Joy:

Celebration in the Midst of Pain

No matter how much we desire perfection and completeness, we need to embrace the fact of our limitations. In our broken world, things are less than what we would like them to be. And our own imperfections are written large on all that we do. This need not drive us to despair. Nor should it prevent us from purposeful activity. We can still do what we must, even when a totally satisfactory conclusion eludes us.

Nouwen reminds us that "there is no such thing as clear-cut pure joy."[74] Our experience of love, no matter how loyal or ecstatic, is marked by selfishness and pain. Even our spiritual experiences do not yield the fruit of perfection. These experiences are frequently marred by doubt and guilt.

Such is our lot. We reach for the sky, but cannot inherit the earth. We long for the good, but frequently produce something that is a pale version of our best intentions. We are like a beautiful princess with feet of clay or like a powerful prince with a physical impediment. Made for God's highest intention, we sometimes fritter away our calling and opportunities. Made for greatness, we easily become sidetracked by our success and power. A profound sadness thus underlies our life.

But our sadness can be turned into joy. This is not a joy that comes from a perpetual striving, but a joy that comes in the midst of our pain. It's the joy of being loved in spite of our imperfections. It's the joy that comes from forgiveness. It's the joy that comes as a gift that we don't deserve. It's the joy that comes as a surprise in spite of ourselves.

Thus, in the midst of our pain we can celebrate. In the midst of our broken world we can still dance.

To Live Again:

Future Hope and Present Experience

While our present experience is frequently less than what we would like it to be, we do continue to look forward in hope. We dream new dreams. Make new plans. Embark on new projects. Enter into new liaisons. Even when our present experience has been difficult or disastrous or full of grief, we are usually able, after grieving through our pain, to live again.

We may not live in quite the same way as before. Loss has a way of affecting us. It can narrow the generosity of our heart. It can make us too self-protecting and too careful. It can also make us complaining and bitter. But depending on our creative response, it can also make us more sensitive, helpful, and generous of heart.

Part of that creative response is to continue to hope in the face of loss and difficulty. We can hope that there is a future for us, even though the present seems so dark. We can hope that our pain and difficulty are not the last word, for not only can our circumstances become different, but we can change as well.

Nouwen comments that a person "without hope in the future cannot live creatively in the present."[75] This does not mean that hope acts merely as a drug that numbs us to present difficulty because our eyes are on the beyond. In fact, the opposite is the case.

Hope allows us to face the present, no matter how difficult our present may be. Hope helps us to see the present with new eyes, with eyes that see how things can be different. And hope can then propel us forward, for we see what we can be, rather than seeing only what is here and now.

Celebration:

Appreciating All of Life

We all have experienced those special events in our lives that are truly memorable. These have been deeply etched on our minds and make us warm and teary-eyed when we recall them. A particular birthday. A special experience with another person. A wonderful holiday. The birth of a child. The list could be endless.

But our lives are hardly made up of a continuum of special events. They form the exception to life, which ordinarily is very pedestrian and prosaic. Much of what we do is repetitive. And even what might appear to be exciting to someone else is for us often lackluster. As a consequence, celebration is hardly the keynote of our lives. It usually only has the character of the occasional.

Yet it can and should be more central. Being thankful should undergird all of our lives and not simply become an expression for what is special. We should learn to appreciate all of life. And this includes light and shadows, sun and rain, joy and trial. Celebration, similarly, should not occur only at the high points and in the good times. Nouwen reminds us that "celebration lifts up not only the happy moments, but the sad moments as well."[76] Celebration is not simply concerned with rejoicing in the good life. It is also concerned with rejoicing in life itself, even when it is marked by trial.

Celebration is not simply rejoicing in the gifts we receive; it is also a matter of rejoicing in the Giver, even when He comes empty-handed. Celebration affirms our being and not only our well-being. As such, it enriches and deepens every part of life.

The Practice of Solitude:

Facilitating the Discipline of Quiet Reflection

There are many obstacles to the practice of solitude. They include the pressures of our external world and the restlessness and compulsions of our own inner world. We therefore need to facilitate the discipline of solitude. Nouwen notes that "there are too many reasons not to be alone. Therefore we must begin by carefully planning our solitude."[77] We cannot rely on our spontaneity.

Nor is there an ideal time or place. Instead, we need to carve out some time for ourselves in the face of many demands and create a place, or several places, in spite of our crowded and noisy environment. For some, that time can best be found in the morning. Others use their lunchtime. Some prefer certain evenings. A quiet spot in the house or in the garden, or a walk along some quiet streets or through a park, or a closed office door, or a church sanctuary can provide the place that in time will become comfortable and important for us.

The importance of time and place is that these can bring some regularity in our times of quiet reflection. This regularity establishes a tradition for our personal life. It overcomes the need to make a new decision each time we wish to spend time in solitude. With that decision made, we are already partway there. We have already created space and room for ourselves.

This is not to say that with space and room, everything will follow smoothly. To have a quiet place does not mean that we will have a quiet time. There are also the distractions of the quiet place. Our restless senses, a feeling of futility, a lack of quick results, and fears in truly facing ourselves can all invade the quiet place.

But before we capitulate to these pressures, we need to give ourselves a much longer time. There are no quick results in the quiet place. It is in the ensuing months that small green shoots will begin to appear on a frequently blighted or barren personal landscape. Because they usually will not appear in a matter of days or weeks, patience and persistence will need to be a part of the practice of solitude.

Being Alone With:

Practicing the Presence of God

Solitude is not simply a quiet time and place. It is not only a matter of stilling the many inner voices so that we can come to a point of quietness and inner peace. It is much more than that. Nouwen reminds us that, for the fourth-century Desert Fathers, solitude was not simply a matter of "being alone, but [of] being with God."[78]

Solitude is thus not only a place of aloneness. It is also the place of companionship and fellowship. It is not only a place of stillness. It is also the place for conversation. Solitude is not withdrawal in order to get away. It is withdrawal in order to be with Someone who normally gets crowded out of our lives.

But it is being with this Someone in particular ways. We can be with God in our active serving. We can be with God in corporate worship. We can also be with God through attentive study of the Scriptures.

In solitude we are with God in a different way. We are there not so much to be blessed as to be still. We are there not to seek answers, but to seek companionship. We are there not to get, nor to give, but to be attentive. Solitude allows us to practice the presence of God as attentive listeners and as companions who are at peace in each other's company.

Many creative and wonderful things might flow out of this interaction. But these are not the reasons for seeking solitude. Solitude is entered into for its own sake. It is the place without demand and expectation. It is the place of love and trust. It therefore puts presence before action and seeks companionship before help.

Solitude:

The Way to a New Attentiveness

In solitude we not only come to peace and quietness, but also to a new attentiveness. In this openness, we are seeking to hear new stirrings within our being. Stirrings that seek to find the light of our understanding.

At the same time, we are seeking to hear the voice of the Spirit within us. It is not easy to distinguish between the voice within and the voice of the Spirit. Hearing the voice within runs the risk of monologue. We only hear the accepted and the familiar. Hearing the voice of the Spirit runs the danger of a threatening dialogue. We only hear the unfamiliar and therefore experience the Spirit as demanding and challenging.

In actual fact, both the voice within and the voice of the Spirit can be experienced as familiar and as other. This leads to true understanding, for we cannot hear things that are so strange that they make no sense. We can only hear things that are familiar and yet contain new possibilities. In this way we can come to new insights and to new commitments.

The challenge in solitude is to avoid hearing only what we want to hear. We need to resist the temptation to provide our own answers. We are seeking our own answers when we fail to be open and when we simply come up with our own agendas.

Nouwen says that in solitude, "our temptation is to do something useful: to read something stimulating, to think about something interesting, or to experience something unusual."[79]

But this is frequently the unusual for its own sake or as a diversion. It springs from the fear of coming empty-handed. We can find ourselves filling our solitude with our own preoccupations and frequently come away with having only what we already possessed. It is when we give up our own agendas that the place of solitude can become the place of inner renewal and new insights.

Prayer and Hope:

The Prayer That Leads to Partnership

We have suggested that solitude has primarily to do with developing a new attentiveness. Thus, listening lies at the heart of the practice of solitude. But good listening involves conversation. In conversation what one hears can be questioned, elaborated upon, made more specific, and made more applicable to our situation.

This type of conversation highlights one form of prayer. This is not the prayer of adoration, nor that of thanksgiving, nor that of supplication. It is the prayer that probes and looks for greater light. It is the prayer that goes on seeking because it is not satisfied that it has understood all that needs to be grasped.

While Nouwen's assertion that "every prayer is an expression of hope"[80] is true, the prayer that probes is particularly the prayer of hope. Its hope is not that it expects God to intervene marvelously and to change situations miraculously. Its hope is very different. Its hope lies in gaining a sense of what is on God's heart. It seeks to understand God's purposes. It seeks to enter into God's concerns and obediently to discern His will. It does this because it believes that in doing the will of God, our life will find its true purpose and this world will become a better place.

This form of prayer, which probes and questions in order to understand more clearly, is the prayer that believes in partnership. It sees us linking our concerns, priorities, and activities with God's intention, and thus lives in the hope that God's kingdom will be more fully reflected in our world.

Action and Hope:

Sustaining Purposeful Activity

Hope is not just a vague feeling that somehow things will become better. Hope involves action, and action is what moves us toward the things we hope for. Hope inspires action, and action begins to realize our hopes.

But not all action is helpful or constructive. Action born of frustration or compulsion seldom achieves positive results. While this form of activity may be characterized by initial energy and promise, it quickly fades or becomes sidetracked. Neither frustration nor compulsion is a good motivation for the long journey of positive and constructive action.

Action inspired by guilt or duress is not helpful either. Action as therapy, embarked upon to rid us of a sense of guilt, becomes action that soon looks away from achieving the general good. It finally becomes self-seeking and self-serving, for it only looks to what it can do for us.

Action under duress is limited action as well. Before long, resentments will cause us to abandon the things we are made to do, and we will begin to subvert the system in some way.

Purposeful action should not spring from frustration, compulsion, guilt, or duress. It should come from freedom and hope. And hope will be all the more significant and powerful when the eye of faith can see its final realization.

Nouwen reminds us that action "is not a fearful

attempt to restore a broken order." Such action assumes too much, for we are not sufficiently wise and all-seeing. And we would never be able to sustain our action in order to achieve such a monumental outcome. We would become overwhelmed in the attempt.

Instead, as Nouwen rightly reminds us, action "is a joyful assertion that in Christ all order has already been restored."[81] Such action works out of a final promise, not toward such a promise. It springs from a believed goal, rather than making such a goal believable. Such hope not only inspires our action, but makes it sustainable.

Power over Power:

Discovering the Power of Weakness

There is something very satisfying about enjoying the fruit of our labor. It is very satisfying to find ourselves at the top or in a prominent position of an organization after having started at the bottom. It is very satisfying to establish a reputation, whether that be as an executive, a problem solver, a speaker, a writer, or a community worker.

It is also very satisfying to have enough financial resources not only to be able to do what we must, but also to be able to do what we fancy from time to time. To have power, status, position, and money sits very well with us.

But there is a downside to all of this. These privileges can so captivate us that they become the controlling factors of our lives. As such, they prevent us from making the hard choices that involve our integrity, our need to continue to grow as persons, and the challenge of serving the wider community, even at the cost of our own securities. Nouwen confides this to us: "Too often I look at being relevant, popular and powerful as ingredients for an effective ministry. The truth, however, is that these are not vocations but temptations."[82]

Not everyone makes this discovery. We are more inclined to think that our position, status, and reputation will enhance our effectiveness, whether that be in "secular" employment or "spiritual" ministry. For, by virtue of our successes, don't we get opportunities that we would never get otherwise?

There clearly is some truth to this. But there are also powerful temptations. Ambition, self-adulation, and power can also corrupt us. These make us self-seeking more than God-centered and self-serving rather than others-concerned.

The key issue in all of this is to gain power over power. In other words, we need to gain control over our successes to the point of holding them in open hands and being prepared to relinquish them. We need to be prepared to journey beyond our securities and experience powerlessness in order to make the startling discovery that ministry can also come out of weakness, and not simply out of strength.

Preoccupied:

Freeing Ourselves from the Expectations of Our Age

Unless we are aged, infirm, retired, or have opted out of life, we are more than occupied. Careers, plans, responsibilities, and duties all fill our lives. Even those who have adopted a spiritual vocation and are seeking to lead others into the rhythm of the inner life, into the art of prayer, and into the discipline of solitude find themselves with busy schedules of administration, teaching, and counseling.

Our minds are busy. Our hands are full. Demands are multitudinous. Opportunities beg for the taking. And we find ourselves driven to do more, even when our resources are limited. Much of what we do does not come from overflow. It comes from wringing out of ourselves the last vestiges of energy.

However, we are not only occupied; we are also preoccupied. Not only the present, but also the future provides no space or room for us. As Nouwen points out, "To be preoccupied means to fill our time and place long before we are there."[83] Thus present activities are already overlaid with future expectations.

When we begin to probe the question, "Why are we like this?" we soon discover that lack of time is not the issue. Nor is our physical survival at stake. We don't do as much as we do simply to prevent mice starving in front of our food pantry. Nor is being afraid of being alone and the fear of being still the only issue—although that may be a part of it, for we do these so infrequently. Much closer to home is the fact that our society values activity and productivity. And we have come under its powerful spell.

Consequently, the wise person is not preferred to the productive person. Inner values are not preferred to laudable achievements. Prayer is not preferred to activity. The "fruit of the Spirit" is not preferred to spiritual exploits. As a result, priests in fact operate as social workers. Ministers in reality are administrators. Prayer becomes doing. And spirituality becomes service.

The urgent challenge for our time is that we again become our own persons, that we develop our inner life, and that we find fresh ways to be nurtured by the God of all consolation, whose voice we need to hear and obey. Out of this will come new ways of doing and serving, instead of the compulsive activity that so readily conforms to society's prevailing values.

Busy and Bored:

Recapturing the Meaning of Daily Work

Being busy is our way of life. Being preoccupied and focused on doing even more is an expression of the compulsions that drive us. But being bored in spite of our much-doing is a tragedy of enormous proportions. Nouwen observes that we in the First World are "busy and bored at the same time."[84] Our many activities do not seem to bring us much fulfillment. There seems to be little joy in our much-doing. And we seem to be given more to complaining about all that we have to do. We do this even while we plan to take on more.

Therefore our work does not enrich us. It does not make us thankful. We don't rejoice in the things we make and the goals we achieve. We are not thankful for the gifts and skills we can utilize in our daily work. We don't celebrate the opportunities that we have to work cooperatively with others.

Work is seen as a burden or as the means by which we earn money to do the things we really enjoy. We live for the weekend. The holiday. Our long service leave. Our retirement. As a result, the working hours of our life are relegated to irrelevance.

Clearly, this part of our lives needs to be redeemed. It needs to be recaptured as having meaning and as a way of bringing fulfillment. While for some this may be achieved by a change of vocation, for most of us something more fundamental needs to take place. This has to do with learning to celebrate the ordinary. With joining faith and daily work. With reclaiming our vocation as part of our spirituality. It has to do with recognizing that our attitude toward our work has a great deal to do with the persons we are becoming and the world we are shaping.

Appreciation:

Having Eyes to See What We Have Been Given

The gentle touch of a friend. The surprise birthday party. An exhilarating mountain climb. A wonderful meal. A quiet walk. A stimulating conversation. The sheer audacity of autumn colors. A mother's care. A mellow sunset. A lover's passion. A moment of solitude. A gripping book. An inspiration. Appropriate timing in doing good. A sense of God's presence. Mad hilarity with friends. A stimulating project. Receiving an unexpected gift. Worship. Play. Prayer. Silence. Work. Love. Peace. Friendship. Family.

As we allow our minds to wander over the many facets of our lives, we cannot but be amazed. Here and there are the marks of love, the signs of goodness, the indications of grace. Here and there are the gifts of compassion, the fruit of service, the signs of hope, the blessings undeserved. Nouwen gently reminds us that "every time we experience real goodness or gentleness we know it is a gift."[85] He is right.

But we need eyes to see and a heart to appreciate what has been given to us. We can rush past. We can be so bent on wanting more through comparing ourselves with others that we fail to enjoy the good that has already been placed in our hands.

Appreciation cannot be an occasional afterthought. It is a way of life in which the present is celebrated and the giver thanked, where we live with a sense of amazement that so much has been placed into such undeserving hands.

Adoration:

Celebrating God's Uniqueness

Meditation has everything to do with development of the self. It seeks to make us more reflective. More aware of the inner stirrings within our being. More sensitive to the voice of the Spirit. More open to new possibilities. Less fearful. Less driven. And more prayerful.

But meditation is not simply about the development of the self; it is also a communion with the God of all grace. It seeks to develop an intimacy with the One who loves us. At the heart of this intimacy lies the art of adoration. Here thankfulness becomes appreciation. Asking becomes silence. Prayer becomes worship. Seeking becomes adoration. Questioning becomes listening. And fear turns to faith.

Nouwen reminds us that "to adore is to be drawn away from my own preoccupations into the presence of Jesus."[86] While admiration is an appropriate response to our fellow human beings, adoration is a response that belongs to God alone. In adoration we celebrate God's uniqueness and otherness and say, "We give You the honor and love that are Your due. We praise You as Creator and Redeemer. We praise You as the great Reconciler. We praise You as the pursuing Lover. We praise You as the very source of our life."

Being Led:

Walking in God's Will

Life is not simply a matter of self-determination. We soon discover that what we think is best or important constitutes a very limited perspective. Therefore we need to seek advice and to be open to the input of others. Our ideas need to be formed within the context of consultation.

The growth of spirituality is also not simply a matter of self-effort. It is a matter of communion. It is drawing on the wisdom of others who have walked the road of spiritual growth and of learning from the Spirit within. Spirituality blossoms not simply from self-effort, but also from being led. It has to do with surrender and with hearing things that we have not thought of and that may even cut across previous aspirations or expectations.

This brings us to the very heart of spirituality and to the significance of prayer and meditation. Spirituality has to do with personal development and fulfillment. But not in the way that we determine. Nouwen rightly points out that in prayer we "have to stretch out our hands and be led to places where we would rather not go."[87]

Spirituality, therefore, knows the hard and the lonely road. It knows the cost of relinquishment. It knows what it means to be led and knows what it costs to walk in God's will.

In walking that road, we often don't feel blessed. We may even wonder whether we have been abandoned. But in time we will come to see that it was the royal road to life and that we would not have grown in the way we have if we had not listened.

Thus, growth in spirituality is not always a steady path that leads directly to greater self-fulfillment. It is also the road of faith, the path of risk-taking, the way of hard decisions. It may appear to be a side track, but it leads us to new life.

The Fruitful Life:

The Matter of Vulnerability, Gratitude, and Care

We want our lives to be meaningful and to have purpose. We also desire to have some impact for good on others and on our world. We want our lives to be fruitful. Fruitfulness, however, is very differently understood by different people.

Some see a life given to prayer as a fruitful life. Others see a life given to social activism and to caring for the poor as a fruitful life. Some see it in terms of healing. Others see it in terms of a successful and important secular career. Some see it in terms of virtue, others in terms of productivity. Clearly we will measure fruitfulness differently, depending on the values we hold.

Nouwen, however, probes beyond these differences to ask the question: What constitutes the fruitful life? Surprisingly, he tells us that the "three aspects of the fruitful life [are] vulnerability, gratitude and care."[88] We would most likely have expected him to say something quite different.

We often think of the fruitful life as springing from strength, power, and overflow. But we soon learn that we often have more to give when we are open, vulnerable, and aware of our own limitations.

Fruitfulness, moreover, is enhanced when our lives are characterized by thankfulness, appreciation, and gratitude. This allows us to appropriate the good that comes our way. So much of what could nurture us is carelessly thrown away because we don't appreciate and appropriate the many little blessings we receive. Instead, we are often unthankful; we grumble and are so focused on future expectations that we don't see the daily good that so unexpectedly comes our way.

Finally, fruitfulness is sustained by care. We need to watch over the seeds of hope. We need to care for what we are and have. We need to channel our resources. We cannot be haphazard or wasteful or slothful and expect to be fruitful. The nourishing sources of life need to be constantly tapped, lest we find ourselves in a position where much is expected of us while we have little to give.

Offering Our Gifts:

Each Has a Part to Play

We are sometimes overwhelmed by people who seem to be so capable and appear to have so much to give and to contribute. We may come across such people in the workplace, the sporting club, the community organization, and the church. Sometimes a member in our family seems to be so much more gifted, and, even closer to home, our marriage partner may seem to have skills and abilities that leave us feeling second-rate or even quite useless.

In spite of these feelings of negativity, we need to realize that we can all play a part, can all contribute, and can all bring something from our unique life experience.

Nouwen affirmingly notes that "we all have gifts to offer and a need to receive."[89] One may be able to offer warmth, while the other contributes discipline. One may provide sensitivity, while the other provides direction. Some are good managers. Others are creative. Some can provide stability, others openness and flexibility. Some dream. Others lead. Some provide a presence. Others possess a practical wisdom. The possibilities are endless.

But when those with particular gifts, abilities, and functions are prepared to harmonize with others who have differing contributions to make, then purposeful activity becomes a possibility, beauty comes into view, and the magic begins.

Thus those who seem to be so sure of themselves need to invite the gift of the other. And those who are more timid need to contribute their part so that a greater good may emerge.

Beyond the Helping Technologies:

Being Neighbor to Another

Our Western society abounds with professional helpers. Psychiatrists, social workers, personal therapists, and dozens of other categories could be mentioned. Each plays a specialized role. And each can contribute something to the healing and help that so many are seeking.

But specialists don't necessarily hold all the answers to our ills. Usually more is needed. And here we begin to touch on the big questions of meaning, hope, and purpose that are so essential to our well-being. It is at this point that we can all play a part. By being neighbor to the other person, by being welcoming and hospitable, by journeying with the other person, and by being affirmative and encouraging, we can reflect hope to others. Nouwen observes that "in our world of loneliness and despair, there is an enormous need for men and women who know the heart of God, a heart that forgives, that cares, that reaches out and wants to heal."[90]

People don't always need a specialist's help. They may need companionship, care, and affirmation. They may need to experience love and reconciliation. They may need to discover that the darker aspects of their past and present can be forgiven. They may need to know that God's love is unconditional so that they are embraced, not for what they have or have not achieved, but for who they are.

If we are experiencing those realities ourselves and are joyfully living life through God's grace, we can be those signposts of hope for others.

This informal ministry invites us to practice the gifts of hospitality and friendship and to provide the safe places where people can experience care and healing.

Remaining Steadfast:

Continuing When the Going Gets Tough

Responsibility, commitment, perseverance, steadfastness. To put these realities into practice is not always easy for us. Particularly not when they have to do with causes that do not directly affect our own self-interest. It is easier to persevere with something that is for ourselves and from which we will directly benefit.

It is often a different matter when we have to remain steadfast in serving others. Nouwen records the words of the murdered priest, Father Stan Rother, who in the midst of the growing unrest and violence in Guatemala stated, "I have too much of my life invested here to run."[91] Rother displayed a steadfastness to the very end.

We, too, need to grow into that kind of stature. We easily abandon causes and projects when the going gets tough. We easily pull out when there are no quick results. We abandon people who don't seem to respond quickly to our help, and we move to other jobs or churches when things don't suit us.

This is not to suggest that we should always stay put. There are times when we have to move on. But we do this too readily and often prematurely. Remaining steadfast may mean being prepared to count the cost against ourselves and persevering until what we had hoped to achieve begins to come into view.

Flexibility:

Finding the Courage to Walk the Unfamiliar Path

While we can create structures that provide some security for our lives, we cannot control life in such a way that we can eliminate the unexpected.

Through a beneficial windfall or, more frequently, through difficulty or even tragedy, life can take a sudden turn. With the latter, our security disintegrates. The familiar contours of our world fade. Faith turns to fear. Answers become questions. And we find ourselves in unfamiliar territory with no road maps.

Most of us find this a very difficult place to be. Some cannot make the adjustments. Nouwen notes regarding such people that "when things went differently than they had expected, or took a drastic turn, they did not know how to adjust to the new situation."[92] Yet adjust we must, lest we lose our way by clinging to a past that is no longer our possession or lapse into disillusionment and bitterness.

Adjusting is a little dying. It is saying goodbye to what is no longer true for us. It has to do with coming to terms with our past while being able to face the future, however uncertain that may be. It involves finding the courage to walk the unknown path. It will cause us to face old fears and to struggle toward a new faith that is appropriate for our new circumstances.

Above all, it will involve making the wonderful discovery that the God of our previous certainties and our familiar world is much greater than that. He is also the God of the difficult transitions and the God of our uncertain future.

Those Fearful Questions:

Replacing Fear with Hope

It is not only in times of transition and difficulty that we ask the fearful questions. In the normal rhythm of daily life, those same questions may lurk just below the surface.

These questions can take many forms, but they have to do with security, certainty, and safety issues. "What if my health does not continue to be good?" "What if I cannot get that particular position?" "What if our marriage does not continue to hold together?" "What if the things I have always believed in do not stand up?" "What if our first baby is not going to be okay?" "What if my boyfriend or girlfriend does not really love me?" We are all assailed by these fearful questions at various stages of our life.

When these questions come, we should not flippantly brush them aside. They can help us to face our situations. They can help us to evaluate where our priorities and securities really lie. They can help us to do something positive about impending tragedy.

But these questions should not become the dominant questions in our lives, for they are born of fear and not of faith. They can drive us to despair rather than lift us to a new hope. Nouwen makes the observation that "once these fearful survival questions become the guiding questions of our lives, we tend to dismiss words spoken from the house of love as unrealistic, romantic, sentimental, pious or just useless."[93]

While fearful questions may stop us in our tracks, it is only words of love and hope that can draw us to new possibilities. More frequently, fearful questions only produce fearful answers. And as such, they will dismiss as impossibilities the answers of love and hope. Thus finally those fearful questions, while they may initially need to be listened to, will have to be abandoned.

Our Spiritual Handicap:

Failing to Acknowledge Our Emptiness

Our age is not rich in spirituality. This may sound surprising when we have experienced major church renewal movements that have focused on new life in the Spirit.

Sadly, much of this has not produced a depth of spirituality with a vision for God, a strength of personal character, a passion for God's kingdom of justice and mercy, and a prayer life that expresses itself in costly discipleship and servanthood. Life in the Spirit has often become a comfortable self-seeking and "me-centered" form of spirituality that emphasizes joy but knows little about growth through trial and difficulty.

Therefore, while we think we have much, we may in fact be empty-handed. Feeling blessed, we may in fact be devoid of God's diverse graces. Claiming power, we may have come under its awesome spell by failing to embrace the power of servanthood, the grace of vulnerability, and the blessing of emptiness. Nouwen has sounded the urgent note that "more and more people are suffering from profound moral and spiritual handicaps without having any idea of where to look for healing."[94] This is true as much for those within the church as for those outside its walls.

This is due to the fact that we have replaced repentance with blessing, discipleship with joy, servanthood with power, vulnerability with predictability, and seeking with success. Our spiritual handicap is that we are empty when we think we are full.

Therefore the time has come for us to start again. To become like little children who are filled with wonderment. To become like those who seek again. To become like those who hear a distant voice and leave all to hear its wisdom.

An Awakening:

Discovering What We Did Not Know

While we may think that we know ourselves quite well, we sometimes surprise ourselves. Unexpected thoughts can assail us and throw into question previous certainties. Unexpected feelings and emotions can sometimes erupt, reminding us that unresolved issues lurk below the surface. We can also surprise ourselves by suddenly discovering capabilities and interests that we didn't know we had.

Nouwen reminds us that "hidden in us there are levels of not-knowing, not-understanding and not-feeling that can only be revealed to us in our moments of great crises."[95]

A major change in our life's circumstances due to a change of vocation or location or due to a loss of a loved one can bring capacities to the fore that we never dreamed existed. Dormant gifts come alive. Suppressed interests emerge. New abilities hesitantly develop. In the midst of change, where previous certainties and securities slip away, a new self can begin to emerge. While we may grieve over what we have lost, we can also rejoice in the new things that we are discovering about ourselves.

The Use of a Word:

An Aid to Creating Inner Stillness

Our times of reflection, prayer, and solitude are not always times when things go smoothly. They can be times of turmoil and restlessness. We are distracted even when we are in the quiet place. Sometimes these distracting thoughts, which flit from one person or situation to another, need to become the very things that we should be thinking and praying about. But at other times these distracting thoughts need to be brought under control.

For centuries, spiritual masters have recommended the use of a word or sentence that is repeated until we come to quietness. Nouwen writes that "a word or sentence repeated frequently can help us to concentrate, to move to the centre, to create an inner stillness."[96] This word should not be an arbitrary one. It should be a word that captures sentiments that are relevant for us.

The use of the phrase "the Lord is my shepherd" can help us to come to stillness. It can also help us to focus on God's role as caretaker, protector, and nurturer. It further helps us to acknowledge our need for protection, care, and nurture. By the gentle repetition of a word or phrase, we can still the inner turmoil and come to that stillness in which we hear things, both old and new, that enrich us.

Prayer:

Giving Up a False Security

The person who prays is not engaged in a flight from reality. In fact, the opposite is the case. The person who does not pray has not learned to acknowledge his or her own humanity and vulnerability.

Prayer is as appropriate as breathing. It is not a peculiar religious ritual for the few. It is the cry of every human heart for meaning, purpose, love, direction, help, empowerment, understanding, hope, and peace. It is the cry that seeks to move beyond what is present to what can or ought to be.

Sometimes prayer reaches out for the impossible. But then, why should the impossible not become reality? Often prayer, however, is more a maintenance exercise. It seeks God's help in the ordinary ebb and flow of life, with its responsibilities and duties.

Prayer can also be transformative. Nouwen notes that "praying means giving up a false security."[97] This is reflective prayer. This is not the cry for new possibilities, but the seeking for a new self. It is not the prayer that looks for God's help, but is the prayer for us to become more open, more true, and less self-assured.

It is the prayer that recognizes that we are not as strong, powerful, influential, significant, and independent as we make ourselves out to be. It is thus the prayer that offers up our own weakness and vulnerability in order to receive new strength and grace.

Community:

A Matter of Heart and Hands

The art of solitude is wrongly understood if it is seen as leading to withdrawal from others. It is not meant to enhance the self at the cost of maintaining concern for others. Instead, solitude is a way to enrich the self in order that we may more fully join with others. Solitude is meant to enrich the practice of community.

While community is the reality we are to live, solitude helps us to live there. Nouwen says that "community . . . is primarily a quality of the heart." It is not primarily a matter of particular structures. It is first of all a recognition that in the faces of other people, I am aware of Christ's call to interdependence, sharing, serving, receiving, mutuality, encouragement, and companionship. Community is thus, first of all, a particular vision of life.

But it also involves a practical joining together. Nouwen notes that "we will never know what community is if we never come together in one place."[98] Heart and hands must therefore meet. Ideals must find a practical outworking. Our dreams of cooperation and sharing life together must be realized with courage and perseverance in an age characterized by independence, self-sufficiency, and isolation.

In the quest of realizing our dreams, we need to make sure that the matter of the heart does not get lost through a preoccupation with the structures of community.

Courage to Act:

Serving in the Face of Difficulty

There is never an ideal time to do anything. We can wait forever if we think that ideal opportunities will present themselves for acts of kindness and deeds of love. We have to seize the day. Grasp the opportunity. Make the most of good times and bad times. There must be a certain reckless abandon about the way we act. We cannot always be careful and calculating. We must do what should be done, even when we don't have the time or when things are not convenient.

Nouwen captures these sentiments in the following prayer: "Let me have the courage to live fully even when it is risky, vibrantly even when it leads to pain, and spontaneously even when it leads to mistakes."[99]

This attitude should characterize not only the way we live, but also the way we serve. Service is never safe. It is always risky. We never know how we will be received and what the outcomes will be. Service is also never perfect. We serve in spite of our mistakes and our weaknesses. And service can also lead to pain. It can lead to the server feeling empty after having given much. It can result in a lack of appreciation. It usually involves carrying burdens that are not our own.

The more we think about all of this, the less we are likely to do. Thus service is an act of courage. It is an act of boldness. It is in some ways a foolhardy thing to do.

Pressing on Regardless:

Service in the Face of Overwhelming Odds

Becoming involved in community work can be an overwhelming experience. There is so much to do. And frequently there are such limited resources. It matters little what area of work we are engaged in — housing for the poor, employment for street kids, after-care for psychiatric patients, rehabilitation for drug addicts, or justice for minority groups — needs always outweigh solutions. Nouwen makes the observation that "here always remains a sense of hardly touching the roots of the problems, of never having the time to do a job well."[100]

But this is no reason not to press on. We can continue even when the odds are against us and we recognize that we are not solving the very problems we are tackling.

However, we need to be careful that such work does not destroy us by making us disillusioned, bitter, or cynical. In order to save ourselves from this kind of negativity, we need to focus more on individuals helped rather than on structural problems solved; we need to distinguish faithfulness from success; and we need to celebrate in the midst of pain and disappointments.

This kind of work brings home to us that we are hardly saviors of the world. It forcibly reminds us how entrenched injustice is in our society. And it can make us into people of perseverance and prayer.

The Matter of Congruency:

Hope in the Face of Imperfection

Reflection should be empowering. It should lead us to new insights and commitments. But this is not always the case. The opposite also occurs. Reflection can immobilize us. It can bring home to us what Nouwen calls "the enormous abyss between my insights and my life."[101] It can also remind us of the gap between our willing and our doing, our desires and our performance, our calling and our achievements.

Sadly, this gap will never be totally closed. We will never achieve all that we would like to do. In fact the more self-reflective we are, the more aware we become of our failings and imperfections, even when others think that we are doing well. This state of affairs has nothing to do with living a lie or being incongruent. It is rather a recognition of our humanity and the incompleteness that we all must endure.

This recognition need not be disempowering. It need not make us pessimistic. It can have the opposite effect. It can make us realize that good comes out of imperfection, strength out of weakness, and blessing out of fragility.

Being Open About Our Inner Self:

Dealing with Our Dark Side

The house of the inner self is not always a place of peace. It can also be a place of turmoil and struggle. One of the things we constantly grapple with is how to sustain our resolve to continue to do what is right. We are all aware of forces within us that pull us away from the good. And within ourselves we can nurture desires that ultimately will be destructive.

Nouwen reminds us that "what remains hidden, kept in the dark, incommunicable can easily become a destructive force always ready to explode in unexpected moments."[102] What is kept in the dark ultimately becomes the dark side of ourselves. What is indulgently nurtured in our inner thoughts finally becomes a part of our being.

While with great effort we may be able to bring these unwholesome thoughts under control, we frequently need to walk the road of humility by opening this part of our life to another person. We then need the help of a trusted friend who cares for us in ways that go deeper than our public persona. This friend must be able to hear the story of our turmoil and to extend to us grace, forgiveness, and peace.

Integration:

Bringing Together Our
Outer and Inner Life

There are two stories to our life: the public and the private. There is the story that is known to our family and friends and the story that we embroider inside our own heads. These two stories do not always coalesce. There can be the public success and the personal inner pain. There can be the social persona of strength and the inner persona of fear and fragility.

It is not easy to integrate the two stories. We often tend to deny the inner story. Yet we must begin to hear its tale and listen to its pain and disappointment. Integrating the two stories will mean that both have to change. The story of strength will thus begin to reflect a new vulnerability. The story of fear will begin to reflect new hope.

Nouwen rightly notes that this attempt at integration will bring about a new sense of wholeness. "We come to maturity," he writes, "by integrating not only the light, but also the dark side of our story."[103] Success and pain, strength and fragility thus weave a new pattern of being that paradoxically does not diminish us, but makes us more sensitive and thus stronger.

Being There:

The Quest for Integrity

Our age—with good reason—has become suspicious of the religious person and particularly of the religious specialist. The latter is frequently seen as someone who appears as publicly "righteous" but is privately morally suspect. In whatever way this suspicion is framed, it finally comes down to the fact that the religious leader does not practice what is preached.

This is a problem for us all. We can be quick at pontificating about what ought to be. Putting that into practice can be quite another matter. This is precisely the challenge for all religious persons. We first need to preach to ourselves. We need to expect more of ourselves and less of others. We need to be converted before we try to influence others to change.

In other words, we need to have some integrity. We can hardly proclaim "good news" if our lifestyle is bad news. We cannot talk about healing if we are not experiencing some manifestation of the wholeness that God wishes to bring about in our lives.

Nouwen puts it this way: "Most of us have an address but cannot be found there."[104] In other words, we might have a reputation, but this does not reflect what we are about. As a group we might make certain spiritual claims, but this is not reflected in our corporate life.

This clearly needs to change. We need to be where we proclaim that we are. Put differently, what we are in our moments of solitude is what we truly are. It is what we do when no one is watching, and how we act when we don't have to perform for anyone, that truly reflects our spirituality, values, and concerns. When we share this with others, we can truly be found "at home."

The Encounter:

Solitude as the Place of Embrace

What is it that we encounter in the place of solitude? Is it only our fragile or impulsive self? Is it the place where we only become aware of the gap between our willing and doing? Is the practice of solitude simply like staring in a mirror where we are reminded of the aging process and the toll that worry has taken on our lives? Is solitude the place where we meet only ourselves?

The answer, fortunately, is no. If it were so empty, solitude would be the practice of despair. Nouwen reminds us that "solitude is the place of the great struggle and the great encounter."[105] Thus we do need to face our fragile self. But we do so in the presence of the Loving Other. We do need to face our hurts. But we do so in company with the Great Healer. We do need to face our waywardness. But we do so in fellowship with the God who reconciles.

Thus, while the place of solitude is the place of honesty, it is also the place of grace. It is not only the place of revelation; it is also the place of embrace.

Rediscovering the Old:

The Practice of Solitude

In the practice of solitude, our primary focus should not be only to hear something new. The new is frequently not the most important thing we need to hear, even though, driven by boredom, we think that it is only the new that can give us fresh hope, direction, and meaning. Driven by this perspective, solitude simply becomes the place of tantalizing new experiences.

The practice of solitude, however, frequently leads us to rediscover the old. Nouwen reminds us that "in solitude, we come to know the Spirit who has already been given to us."[106] In the quiet place, we hear again themes that have long been forgotten. We hear the familiar words of reassurance. Those good but neglected areas of our spirituality resurface.

This discovery of what we already have makes the old new. Thus the practice of solitude has as much to do with the reappropriation of the old as it has to do with the discovery of the new. And it is the living reality of the old more than the excitement of the new that shapes our life.

Do It:

Acting on the Basis of Our Embryonic Ideas

There is a down side to our quest to become spiritually attuned persons: we can become so concerned to hear what our inner voice or what the Spirit is saying that we become more concerned with listening than with carrying out the things we feel we must do.

Moreover, we can become paralyzed by wanting to hear things explicitly when so often the Spirit only whispers embryonic ideas. From the inner voice we don't get fully developed plans. More often we get vague intuitions and, as yet, unclear suggestions.

It is important, therefore, that we be satisfied with this and begin to look for ways by which we can express these undeveloped ideas. Thus the movement to praxis is not from clearly developed plans. Frequently it is the movement from the hunch to trying things out, then to the much clearer understanding of what we should be doing and how we should do it. We need to put legs to an idea, for without working things out in the real world, the idea will not become any clearer. The challenge to "do it," therefore, becomes an important part of confirming our thoughts, ideas, hopes, and dreams.

Nouwen suggests that "setting our hearts on

something involves not only serious aspiration, but also strong determination."[107] It involves not only prayerful consideration, but also purposeful action. Because we frequently set our hearts on what is only a vague shadow, we need to learn to make faith practical by beginning to walk in what is not yet wholly clear.

Displaying the Dove:

Resisting "The Powers"

Not only is our world fractured; it is also the arena of "powers" that bring oppression and desolation.

Such powers include the debilitating rigidity of religious legalism, which promises a path of life but leads us to the desert of forms and structures without grace. Such powers also include a corporatism that argues for a subservience to the program and the goal at the cost of personal integrity, and the claims of ideology that put ideas above morality and concern for the common good.

Nouwen points out that "the world is full of serpents." The "serpent" comes in many forms, not only in sexual deviation and in lack of personal morality. The "serpent" inhabits our corporate structures as well, and evil lies not only with the lawbreakers, but sadly, also with those who are supposed to uphold the law.

It is in this kind of world, as Nouwen rightly reminds us, that we need "the courage to show the dove."[108] To "show the dove" does not mean that we only work for peace, but more importantly that we work for the true and the good. The dove not only signals gentleness, but also purity. What our world needs is not a peace that condones, but a purity that transforms.

Reluctant Obedience:

Learning to Say Yes

Obedience as an important element in religious experience is an uncomfortable idea for us. We find service and worship easier. Service is what we do for the other. And worship is the adoration we give to the God of creation.

Obedience, on the other hand, is responding to what is asked of us. It involves hearing the voice of the Other against ourselves. It involves the call to do what we are not doing. It asks us to be open to change, to adopt new priorities, and sometimes to radically reorient our whole life's direction.

Nouwen, in *The Road to Daybreak*, which charts his journey from Harvard University to service in one of the L'Arche communities, acknowledges that "it is a screaming and kicking 'Yes' that fills these pages."[109] The art of relinquishment does not come easily for us, even when we are long convinced that the time has come to let go or to move on. We frequently languish in the familiar places, even when we have heard the distant voice.

Obedience is never simply a matter of saying yes. That is not its most difficult element. Obedience is also saying no to the familiar. While saying yes to an unknown but possibly exciting future has the lure of adventure, saying no to what is presently ours, even when we no longer fully appreciate what we have, is the most difficult feature of the art of obedience.

Posing the Critical Questions:

Challenged by a Vision of the New

Growth in spirituality is never only a matter of confirming the known and the familiar. It is also a matter of probing the unknown and exploring the unfamiliar. While there is an affirming dimension to our quest for spirituality, there is also an element of disquiet.

It can hardly be otherwise, for we find ourselves caught "between the times." We are located in the now but have caught a glimpse of the future. And it is this vision of the "world beyond" that helps us to pose the critical questions of our present world. Nouwen states, "You are a Christian only so long as you look forward to a new world, so long as you constantly pose critical questions to the society you live in."[110]

Consequently, spirituality has more to do with restlessness than with peace. More with change than with conformity. More with radicalism than with conservatism. More with transformation than with conservation.

Sadly, spirituality so frequently becomes cloaked as the status quo. But this occurs when it becomes captive to the agendas of the power brokers of our society. This captivity, however, can only take place when we lose our vision of the "world beyond" and begin to tailor our life only to what is possible and achievable.

Burdensome Work:

*Finding the Restful Spirit
in the Workplace*

While work gives us the opportunity to gain an income, to make an impact on our world, to utilize our gifts and creativity, and to work cooperatively with others, it is also a burdensome task.

There are many reasons why this is often so. The workplace can be the place of competition rather than cooperation. Because of the pressure for specialization, work frequently frustrates the expression of our gifts. And sadly, work can often bring with it undesirable consequences that do not improve the quality of life and of our environment.

To further complicate matters, we often make things harder for ourselves. Nouwen notes, "I think that most of my fatigue is related not to the type of work I do, but to the false tensions I put into it."[111]

We make things harder for ourselves by pushing ourselves when we are already doing enough. We worry about things that end up resolving themselves. We are irritable when there are insufficient rewards for the things we do. Thus the burden of work is compounded. The potentially joyful aspects of work become submerged, and work becomes a largely negative experience.

While we cannot always do something about the structural and interpersonal factors that affect our work, we can do something about our own attitudes.

If the practice of solitude is to have any relevance, it must empower us to work differently. It must help us to find a restful spirit in the midst of a busy workplace. And this most readily occurs when we take a restful spirit to the workplace, a spirit at peace with God, at home with ourselves and at the service of the other.

Ahead of Us:

The God Who Reaches Back to Draw Us Forward

We have a tendency to put ourselves in the center of our personal universe. From this position we think that only what we believe, experience, produce, and do is important. We may even try to slot God into our priorities as well. In this scenario, God is the one who responds to us because we are the ones who are leading the way.

This picture is badly out of focus. The spiritual life has nothing to do with God being at our beck and call. He is the transcendent Other who is far ahead of us. The spiritual life has more to do with us catching up to God, for we are frequently so far behind. We are so slow to hear. So slow to understand. So slow to yield. And so slow to respond.

Nouwen expresses these sentiments in this prayer: "Maybe you are working in me in a way I cannot yet feel, experience or understand."[112] This rightly acknowledges that God is already there. Already at work. Already gently preparing us for greater openness and commitment. We should, therefore, truly appreciate Him as the One who is ahead of us, but who reaches back to draw us forward.

A Hidden Presence:

Discovering a Trust That Can Wait

God is not only ahead of us seeking to draw us forward into His will and purposes; He is also the God of the past. He is the God of all those over the millennia who in faith look for a better world of righteousness and peace.

However, it is usually not God's anticipated action or His past exploits that give us great concern. It is the present, hidden character of His presence that gives us frequent difficulty. Nouwen tells us that "God's presence is often a hidden presence."[113] By this he does not wish to emphasize that we cannot see God. He means that God's presence is not discernible, not even to the eye of faith. This means that we can feel abandoned. It can further mean that we cannot make spiritual sense of what is happening to us.

In such circumstances, we will hardly attempt to develop a spirituality that seeks to control God. Instead we may discover a new humility and a new impetus to our prayers. It may lead us to a faith without signs and a spirituality without assurances. It may help us to discover a trust that can wait. God's hidden presence is not a nonpresence, but one that awaits a future exposure.

So Close:

A New Way of Seeing

God's presence can be a hidden presence not because God chooses to withdraw Himself, but because we fail to see Him who is so near. Nouwen makes the admission: "I do not see that God is all around me and that I am always trying to see what is ahead, overlooking him who is so close."[114]

There are many reasons for our failure to see, apart from our being so concerned about future projects that we fail to see present blessings. We also fail to see because we are looking for the wrong indicators. We may be looking for peace when God's presence is in the turmoil. We may be looking for resolution when hope lies in the nonfulfillment of our present expectations. We may be wishing for answers when God's goodness is manifest in further questions.

God is frequently closer than we think. We need, however, to develop a new confidence that He inhabits our despair as well as our praises.

Open to the World:

Responding to Need's Plaintive Cry

Openness to the world and its multitudinous and persistent needs does not arise from social activism. It arises from within. And it is sustained from within. Response to need does not first of all arise from need, for many hear need's plaintive cry but fail to respond. Response to need's urgent call springs from hope. It comes from prayer.

Nouwen notes that the one who truly prays is standing with "hands open to the world."[115] In prayer we hear the cry of the world, and in hope we hear the call to social involvement.

Consequently, true spirituality does not lead to a world-denying stance. It does not call us to abandon the world or to withdraw from our neighbor. Rather, it empowers us for involvement. It sustains us in the long journey that seems to have no end point.

Seeking to meet the world's persistent needs will not of itself continue to energize us. A willingness to address those situations needs to be found within. In the place of prayer, with hands open to the world, we will not only gain a vision for action and the will for costly engagement, but we will also find the sustenance to continue when so little seems to change.

Career or Vocation:

Involvement in God's Concern for Our World

Many who are fast-tracking their way along their chosen career path do so with some misgivings. For while their chosen career brings with it particular rewards, it also has its frustrations and disappointments. And at a deeper level there lurks the question: Is there room for service to others in my life or is this all just for me and my identity and family needs? Nouwen observes that "in a world that puts such emphasis on success, our concern for a career constantly tends to make us deaf to our vocation."[116]

The challenge, however, may not be to change our secular career into a spiritual vocation, but to change our professionalism into genuine service. For at the heart of professionalism lies a rigid conformity to a particular ethos and mode of operation, and a commitment to self-interest and privilege.

If we are prepared to embrace a holism that moves beyond these narrow boundaries and open ourselves to the concerns of others, then our career can become our vocation, for the latter will set the tone for the former. Ultimately, living our vocation through our career will be far more meaningful and satisfying than merely succeeding in our career.

Compassion and Service:

Being Sustained from Within

Service does not spring from need. The ability to extend ourselves on behalf of others comes from the quiet place. Nouwen reminds us that "compassion is the fruit of solitude and the basis of all ministry."[117]

Because it is love rather than duty that should motivate us, love's fragile nature needs to be carefully nurtured. The place of ministry will not sustain love's call for inner renewal. For service is love extending itself outwardly to others. Service is love giving itself away. And it is only in solitude that love finds itself again, springing up from within as we are nourished by the Great Lover.

All of this is not to suggest that service cannot also feed us. It frequently does. We can be tremendously encouraged by seeing others helped. But that of itself will not be enough to sustain us. For not only can ministry also be disappointing, but we cannot live off the well-being and blessings of others—not even those we are helping.

Forgiveness:

Changing the Enemy into a Friend

There is little doubt that we wrong others and therefore need to seek their forgiveness. Others also wrong us, and to such we have the opportunity to extend our forgiveness. Forgiveness can be a very powerful factor in human affairs. Nouwen believed that "forgiveness could change every enemy into a friend."[118] It can also heal every wrong. It can convert enmity into reconciliation and distrust into trust.

While we recognize the potential good in every act of forgiveness, we also need to acknowledge difficulties. It is far from easy to forgive someone who has deeply hurt us and who does not come to make things right. It is far easier to nurture our hurt and to inflame it until it becomes a deep-seated bitterness, even though that will only hurt us more. It is also not easy to forgive another when we know that the same hurtful things probably will be said or done again.

Despite these difficulties, forgiveness carries seeds of change and hope. It can defuse difficult situations. It can remove the walls of separation. It can heal our hurts. And always it can not only change the enemy into a friend, but it can change the hard parts of ourselves into places of love and openness.

Openness:

Facing the Sources of Threat

While we would prefer our personal world to be safe and secure, we recognize that it is frequently under threat.

This may not be life-threatening, but threatening nonetheless in that we are confronted by problems we cannot readily solve, issues we cannot satisfactorily deal with, relationships that are not always constructive, a work environment that can be difficult, and a wider world that frequently appears to be in disarray. Little wonder that many of us tend to become involved in avoidance behavior, even though we know that this will not make the threats any less real.

Places of threat should be faced. But they can only be faced if we also have places of solitude. Nouwen suggests that we should "allow the hard questions of life to touch [us] . . . even if they hurt."[119] We can face the hard questions, the unresolved issues, and the things that are threatening if we have first created the places of peace, harmony, and hope within our being and within our important relationships.

Healing the Wounds:

Dealing with the Places of Barrenness

Others sin against us and, by their hurtful words and deeds, wound us. We are wounded not only by what others do to us, but also by what they fail to do. Neglect is simply another form of abuse.

Nouwen points out that "we live in a society in which loneliness has become one of the most painful human wounds."[120] Others can be added. But there is nothing so harmful as a relationship where nothing is given, nothing is asked, and nothing is expected.

This is the barren social landscape where young people grow up in a family where drawbridges are perennially up. This is the place where love is not expressed. Where there is no engagement. No openness. No participation. No joining. No common celebration. No ability to weep together. It is the place where there are no questions and therefore no answers. This place lacks passion and therefore lacks humanity.

There are no easy formulas for receiving healing from such neglect. But there are small steps toward renewal: Facing the pain. Acknowledging the barrenness. Forgiving our parents who were so absent while present. Opening our lives to the presence of others. Finding the areas of feeling, sensitivity, and concern in our own lives in order to activate them. And learning to walk the road of intimacy with all its risks so that we can feel deeply again, love, and be loved again.

Disengagement:

Creating the Place for Reflection

At a particular moment, issues can appear to be so pressing that we literally panic. Problems can appear to be so demanding that they press for immediate solutions. Projects and plans can seem to require only quick resolution. Present difficulties can cause us an undue amount of distress and anguish. And disappointments may appear to be so severe that we think our present "world" may cave in. In the heat of the moment, things can appear in such an urgent and accentuated manner.

It is important, therefore, that we learn the art of disengagement. Putting some space between the pressing issues and the attempted solutions need not be a subtle form of procrastination. It can be the wisest move we could possibly make, for in the heat of the moment we frequently have knee-jerk reactions rather than make considered responses.

With the benefit of hindsight, Nouwen notes that "conflicts that a few months ago seemed so crucial in my life now seem futile and hardly worth the energy."[121]

While many pressing things cannot be left that long, we do need to create a place for reflection before we attempt to come to solutions. And from the benefit of hindsight, we can begin to learn that our anxious reactions in the heat of the moment are frequently inappropriate and wide of the mark. In the place of reflection we may be able to achieve a perspective that has the wisdom of hindsight.

Creating Open Spaces:

Making Room for Purposeful Change

Change happens to all of us. Much of it happens slowly and almost imperceptibly. We are molded by our environment and influenced by our friends. As our society changes its values, we slowly change with it. Physically, too, we change with age.

But we can also be proactive. Change can come because we are dreaming new dreams, making new plans, and actively pursuing new options.

For such changes to be productive, "the first thing we need is an open receptive place where something can happen to us,"[122] says Nouwen. Change arising out of reactions will hardly be helpful, and change to quickly fill the empty places in our lives will hardly be satisfying. Moreover, change made on the run is seldom purposeful.

The powerful possibilities of change first require the quiet reality of solitude. Change first needs stillness, not further activity. And rather than rushing headlong, we first need to create space for ourselves.

The space for thankful reflection on what has been or the space of forgiveness for what should have been needs to be created. And, more particularly, the empty place harboring the fears of loss of significance, position, and power needs to be embraced as the hopeful place, the place of new beginnings. For the empty place can bring forth new dreams, and out of seeing new possibilities, purposeful change can come.

A Receptive Place:

Being Open to Further Growth

Nouwen suggests that "the first thing we need is an open receptive place where something can happen to us."[123] He is right in pointing out that this is what we need. But there are important preconditions that can bring us to this recognition and to the point where we will take constructive action. For we often fail to recognize our needs, and even when we do recognize them, we fail to take appropriate action.

The recognition that we need a receptive place — a place of quietness, openness, expectancy, and hope — usually springs from failure, stress, or difficulty. It occurs when our personal resources are depleted and we are not coping. Thus the quest for the receptive place is often the result of crisis rather than the product of careful management. It comes from difficulty rather than from a recognition of our own finiteness and our constant need for inner renewal.

If we create the receptive place only when we urgently need it, then we can only expect short-term solutions. But if we make the receptive place a way of life, then we can expect renewal, discernment, direction, courage, and hope to be among the wonderful things that can regularly arise within us.

Inclusive Prayer:

The Language of Our Daily Existence

We need to be careful that we do not make prayer a sacred language. Prayer is not only the language of adoration, but also that of anguish.

Prayer is not only the exclusive and often pious language of the sanctuary. It is also the language that expresses our mundane existence. It is, therefore, a broken language. Not only does it express certainties, but more frequently it verbalizes our questions and our concerns.

Prayer, therefore, should include all our experiences of life. Nouwen remarks, "Instead of excluding I could include all my thoughts, ideas, plans, projects, worries and concerns and make them into prayer."[124]

When we do this, much of our praying will initially appear to be a muddle. There is so much that occupies our minds. But in time a certain thread will begin to appear. Ideas and projects gradually come together. Worries and concerns fall away or are transformed into more positive attitudes.

Prayer can act as a wonderful filter. Our anxious, driven, and compulsive thoughts can become a purposeful certainty as we give our continuing prayers the time needed for God to do His transformative work.

Discerning from the Periphery:

Laying Foundations for the Future

The practice of solitude can begin to wean us from the need to be at the center of the action. Having much to give, we can easily begin to think that things will not happen without us.

Moreover, we can think that if we are not at the center of action we may easily become marginalized and irrelevant. Thus we are under incessant pressure to keep up with all that is happening. But in our quest to be relevant, we can easily become superficial.

To move aside for prayer and careful reflection has nothing to do with becoming irrelevant. For in the place of solitude we can see things in a new light. Nouwen remarks that both John the Baptist and St. Benedict were relegated to the sideline. But they "were able to discern better from the periphery."[125]

Of course, if the sideline becomes the place of personal recrimination and self-pity, then it will hardly become the place for new insights. But if we find ourselves at the periphery, either through our own choices or through the machinations of others, we can make the periphery a productive place.

All is not lost when we are sidelined. In fact, the periphery can become the place from which not only to review the past, but also to lay the foundations for a new future.

The Dynamics of Friendship:

Granting Space to Others

Just as solitude is the movement toward inner reflection and renewal, so friendship is the outer movement to involvement and participation. These two movements are interrelated. In solitude we seek to find our true selves so that we can join with others in such a way that we don't lose ourselves and become overwhelmed. In friendship we express the fruits of solitude in order to serve the other. In friendship we bind ourselves to each other. In solitude we free ourselves to be our own persons.

Maintaining both movements is essential for personal development. Solitude without the movement to engagement and service is self-indulgent. Service without the practice of solitude can easily become a trying and demanding routine.

The practice of solitude is particularly important for the art of friendship. In friendship we can bind ourselves too closely. With our demands, hopes, and expectations of the other, we can stultify the potential in our relationships.

Nouwen, quoting Bernard of Clairvaux, expresses the importance of freedom in our friendships: "You can reach me still whenever you wish if you are content to find me as I am, not as you wish me to be."[126] This sound piece of advice identifies that there is nothing static about friendship. We change, and friendship remains vital if it is based on the changing self. If this is to occur, we need to relinquish past experiences and images and gladly embrace the new.

This process of relinquishment is never easy, but it can be made real in the quiet place. It is there that we come to terms with changes that need to be made in order that our friendships may remain vital and empowering.

Spiritual Fatigue:

Learning to Disengage from Spiritual Disciplines

It is easy to get the idea that the more we work at putting a variety of spiritual disciplines in place, the more our spiritual life will blossom. This is not always true. Disciplines can devolve into routines that are no longer life-giving.

Nouwen speaks of suffering from spiritual fatigue and likens it to "being a piece of driftwood on still water."[127] Our spiritual disciplines can exhaust us. We can come to the point where we are no longer inspired by them and drift aimlessly on with little sense of inspiration, purpose, and direction.

We can make several responses to this state of affairs. We can drift on, hoping that the winds will blow and move us in the right direction. In other words, we can maintain our disciplines and simply wait for a better day. We can also disengage and give ourselves a break by doing nothing or something quite different. There is no reason why we should not try this course. Spiritual disciplines are a means to an end. They are not sacrosanct. Our life can also be enriched by doing nothing for a period of time. Just as much as work can bring meaning to our life, so can leisure.

Sometimes we need to disengage not only from our busy world, but also from our busy spiritual disciplines in order to gain fuel for the journey.

Through Suffering:

Grieving Our Losses

We may be tempted to think that some lead an untroubled life. But in reality, none of us bypasses difficulty and suffering. This, of course, is not to suggest that life metes this out equally. Nor are we suggesting that we all experience difficulty in the same way. We do not. Some are devastated by it and have to walk a very long road toward recovery. Others seem to be more resilient and bounce back with replenished optimism. But for both groups of people, the pressing question is: What can we learn from this experience?

Nouwen suggests that "finding new life through suffering and death: that is the good news."[128] Christ's death mirrors precisely that message. Suffering may seem senseless, but it need not have the last word. New hope can spring up from the ruins of previous expectations and plans. New life can come from the greatest disappointments.

But this can only come if we embrace the pain of our dashed hopes and grieve our losses to the point of relinquishment. It is at that place, with nothing in our hands, that good gifts will come our way.

Productive Weakness:

Seeking the Physician

Not every form of emptiness is good. And not every form of relinquishment is productive. These are only good if they are transition points, not if they become the end-points of our experience.

The movement from being too full of ourselves and our own activities to a place of emptiness is productive only if we are open to receive new values that make us less compulsive and less self-centered. Emptiness is not helpful if, having rejected the old, we cannot embrace the new.

Similarly, relinquishing power and embracing the gift of weakness can only be life-giving if it leads to a new empowerment that seeks to serve rather than to dominate. Nouwen thus favorably quotes the dictum of Bernard of Clairvaux that the "weakness which is serviceable is the weakness which seeks the aid of a physician."[129]

Weakness that becomes stuck at the point of self-pity or despair will hardly move us forward. But the acknowledgment of our fragility, places of pain, and areas of need, in order that we may find a truer self, is clearly the productive use of weakness.

Being Guided:

The Familiar Voice in Unfamiliar Times

The sense of being guided so that we can come to certainty regarding life's important decisions is often an illusory experience. This is particularly so if we want our guidance to come from the God of all grace, who calls us forward.

Certainty and faith do not always easily merge together. God's voice and our own are not easy to separate. And many of our strategies to receive guidance are contrived and do not work, for God does not respond to methods, but only to a heart attitude that longs to hear and is truly open.

Nouwen suggests that guidance can come at unfamiliar times and places. He writes that we should "understand our experience of powerlessness as an experience of being guided."[130] Our very vulnerability can make us open to new directions. And our disconnectedness from the secure and the familiar can make us open to finding new meaning and purpose.

Guidance is therefore more the gift that comes when we least deserve or expect it. It is the surprise that confirms that God is the unexpected Helper, particularly when we so urgently need Him.

A New Center:

Finding the Intimate Inner Core

We can celebrate the restless spirit, for it can lead us to creativity and to the quest for new understandings and new experiences. But the restless spirit also needs to become the quiet spirit. We cannot be constantly in a state of flux. The search for the new needs to be sustained by the security of the old. The risk of the outward quest needs to be grounded in the certainty of the inner life.

Nouwen sounds the warning that as long as we "remain absent from the intimate core of our experience, we will keep clinging to people, things or events to find some warmth, some sense of belonging."[131] Put differently, the quest of the restless spirit can come from a fragmented self just as much as our clinging to others for security can come from an inner self that is uncomfortable with itself.

The outward quest coming from a fragmented self will not lead to inner integration. Rather, we first need to face the contradictions within and to come to a place of healing and peace. From that newfound center-point we can again venture out and be stretched beyond our present abilities.

Self-Reflection:

A Secret for Appropriate Role Modeling

Most of us would like our lives to have some impact on others. For some, the circle of impact may simply be the family. For others, it may be much wider. They may become the moral leaders for a whole group of people or even a whole nation. When we think of the latter, we immediately think of people like Gandhi, Martin Luther King Jr., Mother Teresa, and Desmond Tutu.

We will readily acknowledge that the privilege of exercising an influence for good on others involves a commitment beyond mere rhetoric. It must also involve the passion of purposeful action.

But this is not sufficient. Such influence should also involve the power of self-reflection. Nouwen suggests that only the person "who is able to articulate his [or her] own experience can offer himself [or herself] as a source of clarification"[132] for others.

The power of example does not lie simply in great deeds of activism or heroism. It lies equally in the ability to articulate for others an ideology, a strategy, a way forward, and a plan for action. This must tap into people's deepest aspirations and combine realism with hope.

We therefore need to become more self-reflective, not in order to be more inward, but in order to be more discerning. Because the desire to influence others is always fraught with the danger of illusion and the power to control, self-reflection is required to unmask our own pretensions, to purify our motivations, and to spur us forward in true humility.

Solitude in Friendship:

Creating the Free Spaces

True friendship is not only built on the busy round of continually doing things for each other. Such seemingly good activity may in fact exhaust the relationship. The cycle of giving because we have first received can become a legalistic form of reciprocity.

Nor is true friendship built on the busy round of much-talking and constant self-disclosure. The attempt to build friendship in this way may be more a reflection of insecurity than of trust.

The road to friendship is somewhat different. While it certainly involves giving and receiving and open sharing, it also involves a respect for boundaries.

Nouwen notes that intimate relationships that do not create free space for the other can become suffocating relationships. He therefore acknowledges, "I feel an increasing desire to be silent with my friends. Not every event has to be told, not every idea has to be exchanged."[133]

It is in the silences as much as in the conversations that friendship can be built. Friendship should incorporate solitude as much as sharing and common activity. Friendship should not always exist in what we do for each other. It is also what we are for each other, even when we are not doing anything.

Creating Space:

Giving Time for Solutions to Be Found

Helpers sometimes can be too anxious to help. Counselors sometimes can be too quick in problem-solving. And advice-givers are frequently giving answers when the questions have not been properly identified. Moreover, religious people are often only too willing to share their experiences of divine help with others, irrespective of whether the listener has similar concerns or needs.

We therefore need to be careful that we do not push people toward solutions. Solutions need to be found. They cannot be dished out. Nouwen observes, "We cannot force anyone to such a personal and intimate change of heart, but we can offer the space where such a change can take place."[134]

Creating such a space involves giving people time as well as support and encouragement. It allows people to identify their questions, experience their pain, reveal their anger, and expose their dashed expectations. It does not provide neat answers, but journeys with the person at his or her pace in his or her quest for answers and renewal.

This does not mean that no direct help is given and everything is left to the resources of the person seeking help. It means that we offer space, support, and help as it is requested by those with whom we are working.

Vocation:

Serving That Goes Beyond Good Intentions

Natural abilities, gifts, and ideological constraints are all part of the difficult mix that influences us regarding our career choices.

There are always many questions requiring answers as we seek to gain direction for our lives: "What am I really good at? . . . What is really worth doing? . . . What does God want me to do? . . . What opportunities exist in the workplace? . . . Should I only think about my own advancement? . . . In serving others, will my needs also be met?" These and many other questions can press in upon us.

What is clear, however, is that anyone who wishes primarily to serve others must do so on the basis of more than good intentions. Nouwen puts it this way: "Idealism, good intentions and a desire to serve the poor do not make up a vocation."[135] Much more is required and further probing questions need to be asked: "Am I adopting the difficult way because of frustration or guilt? . . . Do I have the resources and skills? . . . Do I have a call to this type of service or am I constrained by idealism or wishful thinking?" These and other questions need to be faced.

The biggest challenge in working out our sense of calling is not consistency in carrying out that call, but certainty regarding what we are to do. For it is this certainty that alone can be an adequate foundation for our consistency.

New Energies:

Finding Endurance for the Long Journey

We can often begin to tire of the familiar. This does not mean that the familiar is bad; it simply means that it has become boring. This is no reason to ditch the familiar. Leaving the familiar place should be the result of careful reflection. And we should avoid the temptation to idealize the new direction.

Nouwen, on leaving Harvard University to join the L'Arche Community, painfully had to discover that fact: "As soon as I left [Harvard], I felt so much inner freedom, so much joy and new energy, that I could look back on my former life as a prison in which I had locked myself."[136]

The experience of change gave him new energies. But this in itself is never enough. For whatever new direction we take, that too has its difficulties and temptations. L'Arche, Nouwen found, could also become a "prison," just as Harvard had been.

Any change is never a permanent solution. Only change based on careful reflection should draw us to new places. This should be coupled with the recognition that no matter how difficult the new direction might be, it is the only path we should now walk.

It is this inner certainty of the rightness of the new direction that will sustain us, not whether or not the familiar place was difficult and the idea that the new is going to be wonderful.

Others' Expectations:

Growing Beyond the Familiar

It is a wonderful thing to live in a context of friends who provide us with stimulus, encouragement, and challenge. This is the heart of community, for in such a context we can serve and be served and grow in our giftedness and responsibility.

But there is a possible down side to this scenario. Within the context of friends, we can also feel the pressure of their expectations. "She has wonderful creative abilities. Maybe she could . . . He has organizational skills; let's ask him to . . ." Or even much more pointedly, "We can always depend on . . . to be the life of the party" or "We can rely on . . . to be strong" or "We can look to . . . for guidance."

There is nothing wrong with our friends knowing our strong points. And equally there is nothing wrong with our serving in ways that are consistent with our recognized abilities. But there is something wrong with being put in a box and with not being able to acknowledge that we are developing different priorities or concerns or to admit that our resources have run dry.

Nouwen, reflecting on his own experience, makes the comment, "Maybe I was slowly becoming a prisoner of people's expectations instead of a man liberated by divine promises."[137] Within the community of friends, we need to guard the gift of individual freedom so that we can all continue to grow beyond the expectations of others.

Life's Mystery:

Being Open to the Surprise

No matter how much life experience and wisdom we have gained, we never come to the point where we have life all worked out. It is too much of a mystery for us to understand its complexity. Nouwen concurs: "Even when we are trying to be in control and to determine our own course in life, we have to admit that life remains the great unknown to us."[138]

We should never lament that this is so. It makes life open. It makes it full of new possibilities. And it puts us in a good position, for instead of being in the place of control, we are in the place of surprise.

If life is subject to our control, then it becomes predictable. If life is so much greater than we can understand, then it becomes open to the reality of mystery. This may at times frustrate us, but it also makes us open to wonderment, prayer, and the pursuit of further understanding.

No Return:

Reflections on Giving Oneself to God

Nouwen tells us that, "When you leave the world to give yourself to God, there is no return."[139]

This sentence prompts a host of questions: Can we only give ourselves to God by leaving the world? Or, conversely, do we only give ourselves to God by immersing ourselves in the concerns of the world? Or can we do both at the same time: immerse ourselves in the issues of our time and yet be sufficiently detached that we do not seek worldly power?

Furthermore, Nouwen's statement prompts us to ask: What does it mean to give ourselves to God? Is this the same as giving ourselves to the service of the church? Or can it also mean a secular vocation? Or is it a life of prayer? Or a life of obedience?

At the same time we should ask: Do we really give ourselves to God? Or are we also self-seeking? Or self-serving?

And finally, what does it mean that "having given ourselves to God there is no return?" Are we bound to our commitment? Will God not let us off the hook?

Each of us should probe these questions and develop our own answers. What is important in raising these questions is that our desire to live with God and for Him requires reflection, prayer, dedication, and the willingness to ask some of the hard questions regarding spirituality and service.

My Own Needs:

Facing Our Lack of Freedom

It is easy to be so involved with the needs and concerns of others that we have no time or resources to face our own needs. In fact, helping others can sometimes be a way of avoiding having to face the struggles within. This, of course, is not to suggest that we can only be of service to others when all is well with us. Nor are we denying that helping others can sometimes be a way of dealing with some of our own needs. But if we are to continue to grow as persons, we not only need time for reflection, but also time for renewal and transformation.

Nouwen embodies these sentiments in a prayer: "Is this going to be the time when you give me insight into the chains that bind me and the courage to throw them off?"[140]

These are strong words. But they are appropriate, for we are less free than we are prepared to admit. We are often still bound by the false values of our upbringing; by hurts and rejection experienced in our past; by our own compulsions and false guilt; by the unrealistic expectations of ourselves or others; and by the unresolved issues in our lives or in our relationships.

The prayer to face some of these issues is indeed a bold one, and the need for courage to do something about these things is a necessary component of transformation.

A Place of Safety:

Experiencing God's Freedom

Life often seems like a long journey with the destination less than clear. We stop here and then there, thinking we have arrived, only to move on again. Sometimes we stay longer in one place. Our neighborhood, place of employment, and spiritual network have been particularly stimulating and encouraging. We believe that this is the place to be.

But we may be prompted to move on, not because we are unsatisfied, but because we become self-satisfied. It may all become too easy and too safe. Thus the safe place becomes the place of danger, for it ensnares us with a peace that subverts the call to adventure and to service.

All the great writers on spirituality suggest that the safe place is finally not to be found in the structures and systems we create—for all too soon these become idolatrous—but is found in faith in the God who transcends all. Nouwen underscores this. He writes that "by choosing us as his preferred dwelling place he invites us to choose him as our preferred dwelling place."[141] God desires to dwell with us. He does not necessarily wish to bless our structures and systems.

In that very fact is the place of great safety, for if we dwell in fellowship with Him, we need never finally be subject to the binding and suffocating ideologies and systems we create.

Models of Life:

The Authentic "Hero"

While we may not carry our adolescent adulation of heroes and heroines over into adult life, we can receive great encouragement from the way others live their lives. This is particularly so when we see them giving practical expression to values to which we aspire.

Nouwen, however, believes we need to model those we would not readily classify as heroes. While he admires the capable person, he is deeply concerned about issues of efficiency at any cost and the issues of power, which lead to the projection of only the strong side of ourselves.

He therefore holds up as an example a quite different model for life. He writes: "Laying down your life means making your own faith and doubt, hope and despair, joy and sadness, courage and fear available to others as ways of getting in touch with the Lord of life."[142]

This model promotes the vulnerable leader. It elevates authenticity above power and influence. It points us away from ourselves as the source of life to the One who is the Lord of life indeed.

The Right Diagnosis:

There Is More Than Only the Problem

Wisdom finds its truest expression not in the form of the right answer, but in the discerning question that opens up new possibilities. And in human relationships it is the art of discernment that is essential to all our helping strategies.

Nouwen comments, "The first and most important task of any healer is making the right diagnosis."[143]

This task must not be seen only in negative terms. It is not simply a matter of identifying the problem. Diagnosis is also a positive enterprise. It also looks for solutions. In fact, the right diagnosis is to identify the difficulty in light of hoped-for solutions. Such a diagnosis may not be arrived at easily or quickly, but a diagnosis devoid of any hope or any answers is incomplete.

In making this suggestion I am not arguing that there will always be complete healing or total answers. What I am suggesting instead is that there is always more than only the problem.

Referral:

Partnership in the Helping Strategies

Seeing that we have limitations, it is at times appropriate to refer someone elsewhere whom we are seeking to help. But referring people occurs so frequently that it is a matter of concern and could reflect something of the fragmentation that exists in the human services.

But there may also be some deeper reasons why this occurs. Nouwen probes one such reason. He notes that "sometimes our referral to others is more a sign of fear to face the pain than a sign of care."[144] Fear may take many forms. We may also be affected by the fear of our own inadequacies. We may readily think that a particular problem is too much for us.

To overcome these hindrances in us, we can adopt several important strategies. The first is that the step of referral can be changed to joining with others. In other words, we don't pass the person on to someone else; we simply invite others to join us in those areas where we clearly lack expertise.

Secondly, we should convert the role of expert and helper to "companion in the journey." The role of expert readily contains the expectation of a quick fix, and such an expectation should rightly overwhelm us. The role of "companion in the journey," while it offers help, also offers friendship and stresses mutuality, not the idea that everything should come from the helper.

Gentle Reminders:

Moving to Integrate Opposites

We are seldom satisfied. When things are going smoothly, we easily become bored. When life becomes difficult, we are quick to complain. This ambivalence seems to be central to the way we operate.

Yet this should not be seen only in negative terms. The fact that we long for the opposite of what we have can give life a new impetus. Nouwen observes that "often it is the dark forest that makes us speak about the open field." [145]

It is much activity that reminds us of the need for rest and solitude. It is quiet reflection that can bring us to the place of social activism. It is loneliness that can push us to search for friendship. And it is in coming to terms with our creatureliness that we seek to understand God's involvement in our lives and our world.

Thus, in whatever state we find ourselves, there are the gentle reminders that nudge us in opposite and counter-balancing directions.

Solutions Without Questions:

Encouraging the Search for Truth

Receiving mere information does little to further a student's quest for knowledge. And the process of learning things without having a real interest in them, or failing to see the relevance of what we are learning, does little to make things a real part of our lives. Nouwen believes that one of the "problems of education remains that solutions are offered without the existence of a question."[146]

Much religious education suffers from the same problem. Doctrines are taught, but they are not the response to issues people are struggling with. Worse than that, in many religious establishments the question is not encouraged. People are given what the religious leaders think is important for them to hear. Therefore much religious teaching is wide of the mark.

In the search for truth, nothing can be more encouraging than to be aware of the issues we are struggling with and to find ourselves with friends who are not only prepared to walk with us toward the answers, but who also ask further questions of us.

Is There More?:

The Journey of Faith

Those who have profound spiritual experiences and those who make sacrificial commitments can easily think that they have arrived. Particularly when such spiritual experiences have been life-transforming, one can readily assume that this is the only way to live.

And where such profound experiences are the lot of people in the public eye, these experiences can easily be assumed to be normal for others. Leaders thus assume that they have answers, not only for themselves, but also for others.

The secret of genuine spirituality, however, is not to remain at the point of our great experiences. Such experiences should never be the terminus of our spiritual journey. Nouwen puts it rather strongly: "Those who think that they have arrived have lost their way."[147]

He is right. No particular experience, no matter how profound, can sustain us for the whole journey. Not even a dramatic conversion or a wonderful vision. For there is little doubt that we will need to be converted all over again and our vision will need to be complemented by further insight as we come to new circumstances and new concerns.

The Gift of Love:

Sustaining Its Fragile Nature

Poets, philosophers, and romantics have all sought to laud, describe, and celebrate the mystery of love. In religious systems, love is usually described in terms of obedience and self-giving to the deity, while in psychological terms, love has to do with caring relationships and a mutuality in which the boundaries of each person are respected.

No matter which way we approach the subject of love, our descriptions will be only halting and inadequate. Nouwen seeks to emphasize the vulnerability of love. He writes: "In love men and women take off all the forms of power, embracing each other in total disarmament."[148]

Love will always have a fragile character. It cannot be regulated or sustained by structures, rules, or commitments. It can only be sustained by continuing acts of love, which are marked by gentleness, care, openness, and trust.

Solitude and Sensitivity:

Seeing Others in a New Light

While we need to be careful not to exaggerate the benefits that flow from the practice of solitude, it is nevertheless a discipline that can yield much good. The practice of solitude allows us to get in touch with what is happening to us. It can make us more aware of our struggles and pain, but it can also help us to see the good things that are happening to us.

Because we are more in touch with ourselves, we can also be more sensitive to the concerns of others. Nouwen suggests that "solitude indeed makes you more sensitive to the good in people."[149]

It can also make us more aware of their needs and concerns. This is so because the practice of solitude helps us to square away our own issues to the point that we are no longer preoccupied with them. This truly frees us for others so that we can affirm the good and care about their pain.

Spiritual Maturity:

Remaining Open for New Possibilities

Sadly for some, spiritual maturity seems to have nothing to do with openness and flexibility. The opposite appears to be the case. Patterns of believing and doing, like the cart that daily traverses the same dirt road, have worn a deep rut. Spiritual maturity has consequently become synonymous with routine, predictability, and certainty, which so frequently lead to pride and hardness of heart.

Nouwen counsels us to see spiritual maturity in a totally different light. "Essential for mature religion," he writes, "is the constant willingness to shift gears, to integrate new insights and to revise our positions."[150]

Spiritual maturity is therefore not a state of having arrived. It is not a condition that is a permanent feature of our life. It is not a commodity that is securely ours. It is quite the opposite. It is, in fact, more fragile. It is being willing, in spite of what we have already learned, to search further and to be willing to revise what we may hold so dearly.

Leading Others:

Pointing to the Source of Life

One of the problems with some fundamentalists—of whatever spiritual persuasion—is that they have things all worked out for themselves and have ready answers for everyone else.

The problem with this approach is not that one should not come to faith's certainty, but that we also need to acknowledge the difficult questions and the contradictions that life brings our way. If we fail to do this, we convey the idea that our religiosity is rigid, narrow, or unrealistic.

However, it is not only some of the fundamentalists who may have difficulty in leading others to a meaningful spirituality. Nouwen comments that many spiritual leaders are good organizationally, but are unable to lead others "to communicate with the source of human life."[151] The problem with both groups of people is that they often have a fear of being open and vulnerable. They assume that strength, certainty, and ready answers are what others find attractive.

They are generally wrong. Those who are searching for spiritual answers are usually at the transition points of their lives. They don't want ready-made solutions. They want understanding, friendship, sensitivity, and the sharing of a faith that can speak about struggle as well as hope, questions as well as answers, and fragility as well as wholeness and strength.

Making Painful Choices:

Setting Parameters for Our Involvement

Every time we say yes to one thing, we may, by implication, be saying no to something else. When we allow certain persons into our lives, we are probably not able to give the same access to others. This is because we cannot do everything and cannot befriend every person we come across. This means that we are always having to make choices.

Sometimes we may make wrong choices, but more frequently our choices are difficult. Sometimes they are painful. For it is not easy to set limits, and it is even more difficult to accept our own limitations.

And yet that is precisely what we need to do and to come to terms with. Nouwen makes the observation that "those who want to be for 'everyone' find themselves often unable to be close to anyone."[152] This does not mean that we should limit ourselves to the one rather than to be available to the many. It means, instead, that in frenetically seeking to help the many, we may in fact be helping no one. For linking up with others as true friend, neighbor, or companion, or joining with others as helper and counselor is usually more demanding than we first realize.

Thus setting limits and understanding our limitations is not so much a matter of withholding ourselves, but of focusing ourselves for true friendship and service.

In the Midst of Life:

Prayer and Activism

We don't adopt the world. It has adopted us. We are in the world's embrace, for we partake of its culture, language, and values.

Yet we don't need to accept all of its dictates. We can live in the world and be guided by a different vision. Not only that, but we can also seek to change our world. This requires strenuous activism and even more strenuous resistance, for the world will attempt to seduce those who walk to the sound of a different drum.

But it also requires persistent prayer, for a different vision of life is given to the one who prays, and prayer sustains those who work for a new world. Nouwen reminds us that true contemplatives are "the ones who enter the center of the world and pray to God from there."[153] A new vision of life does not require the cloister. It can come from the midst of life, but only to the one who prays.

Resisting Evil:

Finding Bad in Unexpected Places

We should never underestimate the power of love. Nor should we ever underestimate what the cause for justice might achieve. Things can and do change for the better in our society. While these changes are usually the result of many factors coming together, this does not mean that the part we have played is unimportant.

However, in being hopeful for change, we cannot afford to be naïve or idealistic. Therefore, we should never underestimate the power of evil. There are always forces and factors that seek to frustrate the emergence of good.

Those forces and factors are never only external. They also arise within us. Nouwen asks the question, "Is there a fatal component of hate in the centre of everything we call love?"[154] This is a hard yet penetrating question. The answer is no.

The component of hate is not automatically there but is always a possibility. In the context of peace, anger can quickly emerge. In the framework of equality, domination can become a reality. In the place of love, jealousy can erupt. And in the cause of justice, injustice can be perpetrated.

It is not a case of blaming a fatal flaw that inevitably destroys good. It is rather that, in the midst of doing good, we can give way to the very evil that we should resist and of which we should most certainly repent.

Competitiveness:

Building Bridges of Cooperation

Our age has made competition and striving into cardinal virtues. The claim is that only those who live in this way will succeed and be productive. And so we pit ourselves against the successes and achievements of others in order to better what they have done. We do so not only to improve on their work, but also to guarantee the worth of our own efforts and, in so doing, attempt to affirm the worth of our own person.

While this perpetual striving is one important element in the manic drive for the new and the better, there is a down side. Competition tends to be the enemy of cooperation, and because competition burns on the fuel of individualism, it can become exhausted.

Nouwen identifies another negative factor: "In a world so pervaded with competition, even those who are very close to each other, such as classmates, teammates . . . colleagues at work, can become infected by fear and hostility when they experience each other."[155]

Such fear not only further undermines the possibility of cooperation; it also undermines our own effectiveness. Fearing the possible greater success of others will not spur us to greater achievement. It only narrows us to a defensive posture from which the great, the good, and the beautiful cannot come. These can only come from the person who is free to dream the seemingly impossible dream.

Conformity or Obedience:

Responding from a Free Place

Most forms of spirituality see obedience as a central feature of their ritual and life. Obedience is not only asked of those who join religious orders. It is also asked of those who adopt particular religious practices and beliefs. Obedience is usually asked of anyone who belongs to a particular group. Members are asked to be obedient to the group's leaders, ideas, and practices.

Where such leaders and ideas are not subject to other criteria and are not open to correction and new ideas, the giving of unquestioning obedience could be a foolhardy activity. Where there are such safeguards and openness, the giving of obedience is an appropriate way to express the group's unity and common direction.

But obedience is something quite different from conformity. Nouwen quotes John Eudes, of the Abbey of the Genesee in upstate New York, who says, "Many people adapt very quickly, but are not really obedient."[156] Fitting in with a group's practices and beliefs may simply be an act of conformity where one responds to the pressures and demands that come one's way.

Obedience is of quite a different order. It is the ability to say a particular yes in the face of options. It is saying yes from a free place and not from a place of pressure. And it is internalizing beliefs and ideas so that obedience becomes a way of life.

Prayer and Activism:

Linking Spirituality and Social Concern

It is easier to be a social activist than a person of prayer. The activist can at least see some immediate results, even though these may be short-term and project-focused rather than long-term and transformative. The person of prayer seldom sees quick results. The social activist, moreover, is usually lauded for the good work done. The praying person is alone in the struggle of faith and the agony of the heart, where no one sees and no one applauds.

Thus prayer is made all the harder. For though we desire to be socially valued persons, prayer is not a socially valued activity. Its pursuit is hardly encouraged, seldom appreciated, inadequately understood, and without public commendation. Little wonder that people with spiritual concerns are great doers, but infrequent at prayer.

But prayer is indispensable for the social activist. Prayer not only sustains activism, but purifies it and gives it new direction. In this regard Nouwen notes that "if you are really praying, you can't help but have critical questions about the great problems the world is grappling with."[157]

If in our praying, we touch the heart of God with its passion for justice and mercy and for the weak and poor of the earth, then we cannot but be given a deeper concern, a larger vision, a more radical approach, and a more compassionate heart for our practical action.

When a Little Prayer Won't Do:

Prayer As a Way of Life

Responsibility and work are central features of our existence. It is harder for us to understand why prayer should also be a key to the way we live. After all, prayer so frequently seems to be the art of managing a crisis or emergency. In other words, we pray when we are in trouble. When things are well, prayer loses its importance.

We can make prayer more central, however, when we recognize that we all have need of insight, guidance, encouragement, and forgiveness.

Nouwen makes the observation that "whenever you feel that a little praying can't do any harm, you will find that it can't do much good either."[158] He is not referring to the prayer of crisis, but to the prayer of formality where prayer is the comfortable additive that doesn't look for answers, but only reassurance.

Both the prayer of crisis and of formality prostitute the art of prayer. For prayer is to be the continuing impulse toward light, hope, inspiration, spiritual intimacy, and renewal.

The God Who Is Steadfast:

God As Faithful Friend

The quest for spirituality is never simply the quest for inwardness. It is also an appreciation of the world and of the God who is beyond the world and yet intimately and paradoxically involved in its affairs.

Our appreciation of God seldom comes by way of doctrinal formulation. More likely, it comes through experiencing God's greatness, goodness, and love. And more particularly, it comes through experiencing God's steadfast faithfulness, which is so different from what we experience in our relationships with others. It is a faithfulness that not only persists in the face of lack of appreciation or indifference, but also seeks to engage us by its sheer winsomeness.

Nouwen reminds us that God's sameness "is not the sameness of a rock, but the sameness of a faithful lover."[159] God as the persistent Lover is an image that brings God much closer than that of the eternal unchanging Ruler of the universe.

Yet both images are true, and particularly that of God as the faithful Lover who is consistently reaching out to us not only to embrace, to forgive, and to nurture us, but also to empower us for acts of goodness in our world.

God and Neighbor:

Seeing a Neighbor's Face in the Face of God

In the practice of spirituality, God and our neighbor are sometimes placed in opposition. The practice of the presence of God necessitates, it is claimed, a withdrawal from our neighbor. It is as if a neighbor dulls the "vision splendid." Spirituality therefore calls us to withdraw from the world so that we can be with God alone.

But this is not really possible. While we need times of quiet reflection, it is not possible to be with God alone. For in coming to God in prayer, we bring our world with us. We cannot leave our neighbor behind as we seek to draw near to God. In seeking God's face in meditation and reflection, we are in communion with the God who loves our neighbor.

Because this is so, Nouwen can assert that "an unconditional, total love of God makes a very articulate, alert and attentive love for the neighbour possible."[160] Because we cannot see the face of God without also seeing His concern for our neighbor, we cannot see our neighbor without being reminded of God's love for him or her.

A Different Drummer:

Hearing the New in the Midst of the Old

Life has its continuity and custom. This is as it should be. But life also tends to be preferential. Not all are treated equally and fairly. Things therefore need to be changed, and tradition, at times, needs to be interrupted and transformed.

However, it is one thing to see the cracks in the system; it is another to find meaningful and long-term solutions. Solutions seldom come from the bureaucrats. They are usually too committed to keeping the system going. Solutions are more likely to come from vision-aries. These people seldom hold center stage. They are more likely to be those living on the periphery. But to be marginalized—either by becoming involved in full-time ministry or by remaining in one's normal vocation but embracing servanthood and downward mobility—is in itself no guarantee of wisdom and insight. More is required.

Nouwen suggests that this "more" involves the practice of solitude and prayerful reflection and goes on to note "that the contemplative life is like hear-ing a different drummer."[161] He is right. In the practice of solitude we are able to dim the din of our world, and in prayer we are able to touch a wisdom that transcends our world.

This of course does not mean that everyone who contemplates will come up with the big solutions for our world. This may be the contribution of only the few. But it does mean that all who contemplate and have the audacity to put the sound of the different drummer into practice in their own lives are already changing the world.

Poverty and the Vision Splendid:

Joining with the Poor

The majority of those of us who live in the First World are relatively well off. Yet there is a spiritual poverty in the First World. Whether this is directly related to our materialism is an open question. It may also be related to the way our whole life is ordered, made secure, and made predictable.

More deeply, it may be linked to the gap we have created between what we believe and the way we live. Having turned a deaf ear to the cry of the poor in our own world and having abandoned a discipleship that calls us away from our own concerns, we may well have lost touch with the God who champions the cause of the poor.

Therefore it is we, rather than the people of the developing world, who need to recover the vision splendid. Nouwen makes a similar observation: "I discovered that the victims of poverty and oppression were often more deeply convinced of God's love than we are."[162]

Possibly one way forward for those of us in the First World who long to rediscover a vibrant and relevant spirituality is to join with the poor, not as helpers, but as partners. In this way we may also draw close to the heart of God.

All in Need of Care:

Acknowledging Common Needs

A rather superficial view of life promotes the idea that there are the bright and the dull, the swift and the slow, the makers and the shakers and the also-rans, the fortunate and the unfortunate.

Such neat categorizations, however, don't fit life's complexity. They also don't fit our everyday experience of life. For the powerful can experience depowerment, the strong can experience weakness, and the less fortunate have particular strengths and qualities.

Therefore we need to be careful about the way in which we categorize others and view ourselves. It is much closer to reality to see ourselves with gifts to bring and things to learn, and with strengths as well as weaknesses. Nouwen makes the helpful observation that "we all are children and parents, students and teachers, healers and in need of care."[163] Thus, while we may have so much to give, we all have so much that we need to receive.

Personal and Universal:

Making Similar Journeys

We always need to be careful that we do not generalize and assume that others experience things in ways similar to ourselves. One person's food may be another person's poison, so we would do better to assume difference rather than similarity because we tend to come at things from very different perspectives.

Having acknowledged this, and particularly allowing for cultural differences, it is still the case that there are things common to all of us. We all, for example, have to come to terms with the reality of death. There are also other common themes.

Our religiosity, our spiritual quest, appears to be another familiar theme. While this may take on a great variety of forms, the quest for personal meaning, faith, hope, and prayer remains a powerful factor in all human development. This being the case, we should strive not only to understand the general and universal nature of spirituality, but also seek to plumb the depths of the personal dimension. Nouwen notes that "what is most personal is also the most universal."[164]

Seeking to understand and to be in touch with what is happening to our own inner life means that we may also resonate with what others are experiencing. The more we can identify what is particularly true for us individually, the more we may discover that others are making similar journeys.

Success:

Resisting Its Insatiable Hunger

Embarking on a particular project and bringing it to a successful conclusion can be a deeply satisfying experience. This sense of achievement is part of the reward for a job done well.

However, when we regularly do well and success is no longer the surprise but the normal expectation that we and others have, then success can begin to become a problem. For when success is no longer focused on the challenge of what we do but on who we are, then success has begun to mesmerize us. Success then becomes the recognition that we demand of others instead of the personal joy we receive in meeting a particular challenge.

Nouwen admits that his success as a writer on spirituality "was putting [his] own soul in danger."[165] The danger is that success can become an insatiable hunger. This results in a drivenness in our behavior and actions so that we achieve more and are satisfied less. This eventually will deeply undermine the very fabric of our being.

When success determines our very being instead of being the happy outcome of a particular project, then success has invaded our inner sanctuary as a despot who mercilessly drives us forward.

Withdrawal:

A Key Part of Purposeful Activity

Life is not only made up of the results of our own determinations and choices. Life's mysterious quality seems to run much deeper than that. But life should not be simply what happens to us. We are, after all, responsible agents who should act into life with boldness and hope.

Being prepared to withdraw from our busy activities and schedules is part of exercising our responsibility. We should not wait until this becomes inevitable because we run out of steam or fall sick. Yet it is usually hard for us to see withdrawal as part of our purposeful response to life.

Doing and achieving good things spring much more readily to mind. For we see doing as building a better future world and withdrawal as merely marking time.

But the opposite can be the case. Doing can be marking time, and purposeful withdrawal can lay the basis for new hope and action. Nouwen reminds us that "human withdrawal is a very painful and lonely process, because it forces us to face directly our own condition in all its beauty as well as misery."[166] In withdrawal we gain space to evaluate and time to reflect. And in that very process we can again come in touch with the good and bad impulses that move us.

In that free space we may well come to clearer strategies and a stronger resolve. But even if we only come to a truer self, we will have gained much for our journey forward.

Under Your Careful Gaze:

God As the Concerned Other

God is not an exacting judge nor an indulgent father. He is neither severe nor lax. Nor is He so almighty that He cannot be moved by our concerns. God is the concerned Other under whose careful gaze we live.

Nouwen confesses God in these terms: "Your eyes are so severe yet so loving, so unmasking yet so protecting, so penetrating yet so caressing, so profound yet so intimate, so distant, yet so inviting."[167] This is a beautiful confession.

Here the issue is not whether God should be called "he" or "she," for He is beyond sexuality. Nor is the concern particular doctrinal formulations, however important they may be. Here the issue is one's personal experience of the One who is wholly Other, yet who is so close. Here we speak of the One who cannot be bound by ecclesiastical traditions, but who draws near to those who seek Him.

This is not the God of the eternal principle or some preexistent entity, but the experience of the One who enters our pain and struggle not as sympathizer but as an empowerer leading us forward to hope and fortitude, grace and persistence, gentleness and steadfastness.

The Mother of Expectation:

Nurturing Our Dreams

If we are not too preoccupied with the immediate and not too overwhelmed by all we think we need to do, we may have the space to do some dreaming. I am not so much talking about daydreaming, but more specifically about intuitive and prayerful thinking.

Some might call this creative visualization. But this does not capture what I mean, for visualization presupposes that one already has some idea of the object of focus. I am talking about the free play of our thoughts and imaginations.

This is a strategy that seeks to think the unthinkable and dream the impossible. This needs to be prayerful. For the product of this kind of creativity is not the result of our own self-effort, but comes as a surprise from the God who is radically beyond the ordinary.

However, we cannot adopt everything that comes to us in this way. Our dreams, hopes, and ideas will always far outstrip our ability to bring them all into reality. Some of our dreams will therefore need to be discarded.

But some dreams need to be discerningly maintained. They provide our goals for the present and our hopes for the future. While some of those dreams may be quickly realized, others wait for the amazing confluence of opportunity, appropriate setting, and God's providence, which make it the "right time." Such dreams, which await future realization, need to be sustained by "the mother of expectation," which Nouwen calls "patience."[168]

True Freedom:

Life Is More Than Its Circumstances

We are always, to a greater or lesser degree, subject to outside forces and moved by internal constraints. The latter has to do with our personal need for security, respect, acceptance, and love.

The power of outside forces has to do with the influence that tradition, ideology, culture, accepted values, and institutional loyalties exercise upon us. When all or many of these factors come together, we may find ourselves subject to oppression, the power of which can subdue the voice of protest and the call for change and reform.

Christians in Nazi Germany experienced such oppression. Yet not all were subdued. Dietrich Bonhoeffer, the Lutheran pastor and theologian-turned-political-activist, was one who raised his voice in protest and put legs to his opposition. He was rewarded with imprisonment. In his *Letters and Papers from Prison,* it is clear that his spirit was far from cowed.

As Nouwen observes, "Amid the most frightful forms of oppression and violence these people [of whom Bonhoeffer was but one] discovered within themselves a place where no-one had power over them, where they were wholly free."[169]

It is not only appropriate to ask what makes men and women like these, but also to ask how we can experience true freedom and live beyond the control of our circumstances. Clearly, it can only be those who have settled their identity needs, who resist the powers of our age, and whose vision of life is large enough to reject the narrow and dogmatic demands of those in power.

Work and Faith:

Solitude Knows the Cry of the World

Throughout these reflections, we have emphasized the nature and development of personal spirituality. But we have also sought to develop a complementary theme: personal spirituality is not achieved individualistically and is not simply a quest for self-improvement.

Spirituality can only fully develop when we include others and serve our neighbor. A spirituality that only knows "holy isolation" is most probably an illusion, and a spirituality that fails to serve others is more than likely self-indulgent.

True spirituality knows both the place of solitude and the cry of the world. It is concerned about self-development but sees it occurring much more through serving another than through pampering the self.

Because true spirituality so fully turns its face toward the world, it needs to be sustained in a community of faith. For if we face the cry of the world by ourselves, we will certainly become overwhelmed.

This, of course, does not mean that the community of faith is always successful in its response to the world. Nouwen writes, "As a community of faith we work hard, but we are not destroyed by the lack of results."[170] The reason the community of faith is not destroyed is that we can exist in no other way. For such is the nature of true spirituality.

Praxis:

Learning by Doing

Much of life is spent preparing for and gaining knowledge for future roles and tasks. And many of our educational strategies are based on the premise of learning first in order that we may do later. For some, this has resulted in much learning but little doing. For others, it has meant quite a deal of unlearning once they have experienced the real world.

Yet it should be obvious that many things are learned by doing. One learns to pray by praying, to serve by serving, and to love by loving.

This is important for spirituality. It can never remain simply at the level of ideas, liturgies, or dogmas. It finds its true identity in the reality of engagement and practical participation.

Nouwen hints at this. He writes, "The great illusion of leadership is to think that a person can be led out of the desert by someone who has never been there."[171] Not only can we not look to spiritual guides who lack life's difficult experiences or who have failed to make sense of them or acknowledge them, but we also need to walk our own desert experiences and learn from them.

Because spirituality does not embrace only an aspect of life, but all of it, all of life's experiences become the testing ground for linking faith and practice. Thus, in being, living, doing, praying, serving, risking, loving, and participating, we are weaving a pattern for understanding our spirituality.

Fragmented:

Overcoming a Divided Self

We live with a divided self. We desire the good but frequently sow the seeds of evil. We hope for the best but make choices that eventually will lead us in the opposite direction.

We also experience life in a fragmented way. Our education may have nothing to do with the job we have. And the natural talents we have may be lying dormant in our present vocation. More seriously, we feel the constant tug of competing demands: home and work, family and leisure, spirituality and worldly concern, career and time with friends.

Nouwen admits: "I have fragmented my life into many sections that do not really form a unity."[172]

It is doubtful that we will ever find a unity by attempting to integrate all the diversity of life. Instead, such a unity can only be found as a hope within our being. It is because we are relatively at one with ourselves and experience something of the love of the One who calls us to intimacy and integrity that we can be at one with our world, because we experience life as meaningful and purposeful. Unity is found when we overcome the divided self by living in truth and love.

Facing our Limitations:

Overcoming the Onslaught of Cynicism

While we believe that we are full of potential and have untapped capacities, we also experience life's limitations. Sometimes these limitations are simply those of time, energy, and opportunity. Sometimes they are the limitations of capacity.

But frequently our limitations have nothing to do with energy or capacity. They have to do with disillusionment, resignation, or despair. In the face of life's difficulties, we have simply given up. Thus we banish hope for the future and face the onslaught of death. Nouwen makes the observation: "That's why we are so deeply affected by life's disappointments and setbacks; they remind us that sooner or later everything decays."[173]

Furthermore, life's setbacks not only remind us of the eventuality of death; they are also death-dealing. They sap our present impulse to do the greater good and walk the extra mile.

Thus we need to face constantly the greatest threat to realizing our full potential—the threat of cynicism that prematurely kills the power of hope.

Transforming Loneliness:

Finding an Unshakable Center

We do not always enjoy the fruit of our success. We can feel quite empty after having achieved a good result or completing a particular project. Similarly, we can feel lonely, even though our friends are present, and we can feel estranged from the God who promises to be near.

These experiences need not bring us to despair. They can be productive. Nouwen suggests that "instead of running away from our loneliness and trying to forget or deny it, we have to protect it and turn it into a fruitful solitude."[174]

The value in these seemingly negative experiences of loneliness and estrangement is that we can rediscover that there is more to life than our successes, achievements, friends, and spiritual comforts.

These experiences suggest that there is a basic dissatisfaction that can spur us to find a new center of stillness and meaning within ourselves that is not dependent on our external circumstances. In finding this new center, we transform our disturbing loneliness into a fruitful solitude that expresses itself in an inner strength that cannot easily be shaken.

Our Own Rhythm:

Expressing Our Spiritual Uniqueness

Nouwen recommends that in the quest for spirituality, we should "try to find our own rhythm."[175]

By this he does not mean that we should not draw on the wisdom of the spiritual masters. Nor that we should fail to seek the advice of our contemporaries who have walked the road a little longer than we have. For our own spiritual quest cannot be made alone. We need the support, encouragement, and challenge of others, even though they cannot walk the road for us.

But we cannot live another's form of spirituality, just as much as we should not live another person's dreams. Finding our own rhythm need not be a narrow, individualistic assertiveness, but the joyous expression of the way God has uniquely made us. It is a recognition that spirituality is not just a matter of routines, but more importantly a matter of intimacy.

Beyond Methods:

Experiencing the Unexpected

Throughout these reflections we have attempted to chart the road of spirituality without providing all the road maps. We have spoken of experiences rather than of timeless principles.

More importantly, we have suggested that the things beyond our own willing and doing and beyond methods are what make life challenging and fruitful. Nouwen concurs: "If anything significant takes place in my life, it is not the result of my own 'spiritual' calisthenics, but only the manifestation of God's unconditional grace."[176]

While various spiritual disciplines can start us on the royal road to a greater vision of life, they cannot sustain us indefinitely. For life is more than methods, and spirituality is more than a composite of its disciplines. True spirituality has as much to do with the unexpected as with what we pray for. It has more to do with the undeserved than with what we expect is rightfully ours. And it has infinitely more to do with God's grace than with the results of our own good efforts.

The Importance of the Question:

Being Open to New Possibilities

We tend to prefer answers to questions. Answers are meant to reassure. Questions usually disturb us. Some, in their quest for a full spirituality, think that answers must be found for everything.

Yet there is nothing as significant as the power of the question in our quest for wholeness and our meaningful participation in the world. For questions ruffle the smooth front of what we already know and open us up to new possibilities. Questions therefore need to be embraced as the potential harbingers of good news. But so often we close off the power of the question.

Nouwen, however, states that we need to live the question. He suggests that "our first task [especially as teachers] is not to offer information, advice or even guidance, but to allow others to come into touch with their own struggles, pains, doubts and insecurities."[177] These struggles are the very issues of life, and to give ready-made answers subverts not only the power of the question, but the quest for life itself.

We may often think that God is only with us in the answer. He is, however, equally present in the question.

When Giving Is No Longer Enough:

Joining the Other's Journey

Those who live in the First World cannot be un-
aware of the grinding poverty that exists in the
Third World. The media has a way of reminding us
about these conditions—a way that probes the edges
of our guilt and moves us to make our token gifts.

We are also aware of the "Fourth World" that
exists within our First World: the world of the per-
manently unemployed, the world of those with
disabilities, and the world of the alcoholic and drug
dependent. Here also we make our limited response
by giving the extra dollar over and above the welfare
dollar that comes out of our taxes.

But those who inhabit the "Fourth World" are not
known to us personally. Their faces remain that of
strangers. We only know them by the stylized image on
the television, crafted to inspire pity. They never sit at
our tables. And we have never clasped their hands in
true companionship.

Nouwen's penetrating question regarding this
state of affairs is to the point: "Why is it that we keep
giving dimes without daring to look into the face of
the beggar?"[178] The answer is painfully obvious: beg-
gars more surely invite us to inhabit their world and
beckon us to fill it with good things. But there must
come a time when giving is no longer enough and companionship becomes the call to integrity.

Such companionship never means that we attempt to become the beggar, the disabled person, or the drug addict. It certainly does not mean that we negate who we are or what we have. But it does mean that we clasp the beggar's hand, break bread together, and join one another in the journey toward wholeness.

Also for Ourselves:

Receiving When We Are Giving

The art of care, the act of service, the expression of compassion, and the practice of active helpfulness are never only for another. They are also for ourselves. Sometimes we gain more than those we seek to help.

In serving others we gain various satisfactions, develop particular skills, and usually gain the commendation of the wider community. At a somewhat deeper level, we gain the long-term benefits of becoming a certain kind of person through the practice of caring helpfulness.

But these by no means exhaust all that we can gain. Far more basically, we can gain sustenance for our own lives from our active participation in the lives of others.

Nouwen suggests that we need those we are serving as much as they need us. He notes: "Jesus speaks through the broken hearts of the handicapped, who are considered marginal and useless."[179] From them we can learn the important lessons of joy in the midst of pain, purpose in the face of meaninglessness, and hope in the midst of rejection.

But they can also give us something more. Participating in their journey can give our life an integrity that brings us closer to the Man of Sorrows than spiritual ecstasy, enthusiastic worship, dedicated prayer, and profound religious wisdom. For the Man of Sorrows seldom appears where we would like to find Him. He is more frequently with those who are at the margins than with those who are at the center of ecclesiastical power.

The Service of Faithfulness:

Being a Window to a New World

Unless we have totally withdrawn from the world, our lives will be a window for other people. People can see what we are about. And it should hardly come as a surprise that others can usually see quite clearly what our values are.

In this sense, we do not live only for ourselves. For even if we never do anything for another person, we do something to other people, even when we don't realize it. Nouwen observes that "[one person's] faithfulness [is another person's] hope."[180]

When we respond to the divine impulse to forgive and to do the greater good, our lives become a window to a new reality. This reality every human being has a desire for but seldom gains a glimpse of.

Because we see the way of peace, justice, and mercy so little, we doubt not only its achievability, but also its value. But part of its value will be realized when those who live for peace and righteousness, while they may not achieve a better world, at least live as windows of the fact that such a world ought to be.

While we may grieve over what we have lost, we can also rejoice in the new things that we are discovering about ourselves.

APPENDIX I

A Brief Introduction to Henri Nouwen

Henri Nouwen is one of the most influential contemporary writers on Christian spirituality. It is not difficult to identify some of the factors that have contributed to his success. Not only has he drunk deeply at the well of his own Catholic heritage, with its rich traditions and practices of spirituality, ranging from the *Desert Fathers (The Way of the Heart)* through the contemporary contemplative giant *Thomas Merton (Thomas Merton: Contemplative Critic);* but he expresses a strong ecumenical vision, having taught pastoral theology for many years at two of America's most prestigious Protestant universities, Yale and Harvard.

But more importantly, Nouwen's most endearing quality is his profound ability to reflect on his own spiritual journey and struggles. In sharing these with his readers, he allows them to share in his journey of faith.

Nouwen once made the observation that "that which is most personal is also most universal." In *The Genesee Diary* and *The Road to Daybreak,* he admirably demonstrates this thesis. Here Nouwen is most self-revealing and universally challenging and helpful at the same time. In *The Genesee Diary,* he struggles with the relevance and renewal of his faith. In *The Road to Daybreak,* he makes the painful journey from a successful career as a university professor to the greater vocation of his call to work with the marginalized in our society—those with intellectual disabilities.

What is universal in both of these deeply personal books is that we all struggle with the relevance of our faith and our vocation, and we all question whether we do the work of convenience or follow the call to do the greater good. That Nouwen constantly struggled with these issues is evidenced by his concern for the poor in Latin America, revealed in *Compassion, Gracias! A Latin American Journal* and *Love in a Fearful Land.*

This deeply personal dimension is expressed in all his writings. While we learn from him the art of prayer in *With Open Hands,* we also meet the praying person in *A Cry for Mercy.* Nouwen writes *Aging,* but also shares his own sense of personal loss through his mother's death in the book *In Memoriam.*

But it is not only the deeply personal and caring dimension that has made Nouwen such an enduring writer on spirituality. It is also his ability to show its relevance for our technological age. Scientism cannot replace personalism. Techniques cannot replace ministry. Rationalism cannot replace spiritual sensitivity. And achievement cannot replace the need for reflection and solitude. In his many writings, Nouwen tackles the myth of self-sufficiency, power, and success and replaces it with the gentler version of interdependence, vulnerability, and ministry. Moreover, he demonstrates that the practice of spirituality is not the luxury of the religious person, but the way in which we can all be more fully human.

For those who wish to go to the very heart of Nouwen's writing on Christian spirituality, *Reaching Out* best expresses his position. *Out of Solitude, Clowning in Rome,* and *The Way of the Heart* contain helpful material on the practice of meditation and the way to achieve solitude even while participating in a busy world with all its demands. Those engaged in active service will be helped by his *Creative Ministry* and *The Wounded Healer.*

Most essentially, Nouwen calls us into the fray of life and away from the holy enclave. But he reminds us that we can only continue the journey and become more truly human ourselves if we are also men and women of prayer, faith, and caring service. And this calls for the practice of solitude so that we can continue to be empowered with new hope, courage, and perseverance. In developing this important practice, Henri Nouwen's writings provide us with stimulus, challenge, encouragement, and practical steps in creating a still point in a turning universe.

APPENDIX II

A Brief Chronology of Henri Nouwen's Life

1932

24 January: Henri Josef Machiel born to Laurent and Maria Nouwen in the Dutch village of Nijkerk near Amsterdam, The Netherlands

1950

Enters seminary in Utrecht to train for the priesthood

1957

Ordained as priest in the archdiocese of Utrecht

Studies psychology at the Catholic University of Nijmegen

1964

Moves to the United States and becomes involved in clinical pastoral education and research at the Menninger Clinic in Topeka, Kansas

1966

Appointed as visiting professor to the psychology department, University of Notre Dame, Indiana

1968

Returns to Holland and for the first two years teaches pastoral psychology and Christian spirituality to seminarians at the Pastoral Institute in Amsterdam

1969

His first book, *Intimacy: Essays in Pastoral Psychology,* published

1971

Works for a doctoral degree in theology at the University of Utrecht; publishes *Creative Ministry*

Returns to United States as professor of pastoral theology in the Divinity School, Yale University

1972

With Open Hands, Pray to Live (reprinted as *Thomas Merton: Contemplative Critic*) and *The Wounded Healer: Ministry in Contemporary Society* published

1974

Out of Solitude: Three Meditations on the Christian Life and *Aging: The Fulfillment of Life,* published

Spends some months in retreat at the Trappist Abbey of the Genesee in upstate New York; his reflections on this experience published in 1976 as *The Genesee Diary: Report from a Trappist Monastery*

1975

Reaching Out: The Three Movements of the Spiritual Life published

1977

The Living Reminder: Service and Prayer in Memory of Jesus Christ published

1979

Clowning in Rome: Reflections on Solitude, Celibacy, and *Prayer,* and *Contemplation* published

1980

In Memoriam, an extended reflection on the death of his mother, published

1981

The Way of the Heart, Making All Things New: An Invitation to the Spiritual Life, and *A Cry for Mercy: Prayers from the Genesee* published

Resigns from Yale and, after a Spanish course in Bolivia, joins the Maryknoll missionaries in Lima, Peru, for work with the poor

1982

Returns to the United States after realizing that he wasn't suited for this type of ministry

Compassion: A Reflection on the Christian Life and *A Letter of Consolation* published

1983

Begins teaching at Harvard University

Spends time in Mexico and Nicaragua, leading to a whirlwind U.S. tour, pleading on behalf of the struggles of the people of Central and Latin America

Gracias! A Latin American Journal published

1984

Makes a thirty-day retreat at the L'Arche Community in Trosly, France, leading to a growing interest in that ministry

Travels to Guatemala to write the story of murdered missionary priest Stan Rother; published under the title *Love in a Fearful Land*

1985

Leaves Harvard to spend a year at Trosly as part of his growing conviction to live with and serve those with intellectual disabilities. This journey described in *The Road to Daybreak*, published in 1988

1986

In the House of the Lord published

Becomes a resident priest at the Daybreak L'Arche Community in Canada

1987

Behold the Beauty of the Lord published

1988

Letters to Marc about Jesus published

1989

Seeds of Hope, Heart Speaks to Heart: Three Prayers to Jesus, and *In the Name of Jesus: Reflections on Christian Leadership* published

1990

After a serious accident, Nouwen writes *Beyond the Mirror: Reflections on Death and Life,* and *Walk with Jesus: Stations of the Cross* published

1992

Life of the Beloved: Spiritual Living in a Secular World and *Return of the Prodigal Son: A Meditation on Fathers, Brothers, and Sons* published

1993

Jesus and Mary: Finding Our Sacred Center published

1994

Our Greatest Gift: A Meditation on Dying and Caring, With Burning Hearts: A Meditation on the Eucharistic Life, and *Here and Now: Living in the Spirit* published

1995

The Path of Waiting, The Path of Freedom, The Path of Power, and *The Path of Peace* published

1996

Can You Drink This Cup?, Bread for the Journey: A Daybook of Wisdom and Faith, and *The Inner*

Voice of Love: A Journey through Anguish to Freedom published

September 21, Nouwen died of a heart attack in The Netherlands and on September 28 was buried in the Sacred Heart Cemetery near Toronto, Canada.

1997

Adam: God's Beloved and *Sabbatical Journey: The Final Year* published

NOTES

1. *The Road to Daybreak*, p. 20
2. *Heart Speaks to Heart*, p. 21
3. *Reaching Out*, p. 23
4. *With Open Hands*, p. 12
5. *The Road to Daybreak*, p. 8
6. *The Road to Daybreak*, p. 21
7. *Reaching Out*, p. 34
8. *Heart Speaks to Heart*, p. 25
9. *The Road to Daybreak*, p. 64
10. *The Road to Daybreak*, p. 12
11. *Compassion*, p. 4
12. *Out of Solitude*, p. 14
13. *With Open Hands*, p. 14
14. *The Way of the Heart*, p. 27
15. *The Road to Daybreak*, p. 29
16. *The Road to Daybreak*, p. 81
17. *The Wounded Healer*, p. xv
18. *The Road to Daybreak*, p. 68
19. *The Road to Daybreak*, p. 141
20. *Reaching Out*, p. 37
21. *The Road to Daybreak*, p. 84
22. *The Road to Daybreak*, p. 56
23. *Heart Speaks to Heart*, p. 51
24. *The Way of the Heart*, p. 20
25. *The Road to Daybreak*, p. 193
26. *Out of Solitude*, p. 22
27. *Reaching Out*, p. 41

58. *Heart Speaks to Heart,* p. 29
59. *The Way of the Heart,* p. 24
60. *Out of Solitude,* p. 55
61. *The Wounded Healer,* p. 84
62. *Out of Solitude,* p. 21
63. *The Way of the Heart,* p. 64
64. *The Wounded Healer,* p. 82
65. *The Wounded Healer,* p. 93
66. *The Road to Daybreak,* p. 222
67. *In the Name of Jesus,* p. 16
68. *With Open Hands,* p. 100
69. *With Open Hands,* p. 70
70. *With Open Hands,* p. 46
71. *The Road to Daybreak,* p. 89
72. *In the Name of Jesus,* p. 45
73. *In the Name of Jesus,* p. 42
74. *Out of Solitude,* p. 52
75. *Out of Solitude,* p. 59
76. *In the House of the Lord,* p. 66
77. *Making All Things New,* p. 71
78. *The Way of the Heart,* p. 69
79. *Making All Things New,* p. 76
80. *With Open Hands,* p. 76
81. *In the House of the Lord,* p. 27
82. *In the Name of Jesus,* p. 71
83. *Making All Things New,* p. 25
84. *Making All Things New,* p. 30
85. *In the House of the Lord,* p. 43
86. *The Road to Daybreak,* p. 71
87. *In the Name of Jesus,* p. 71

88. *In the House of the Lord*, p. 40
89. *In the House of the Lord*, p. 48
90. *In the Name of Jesus*, p. 24
91. *Love in a Fearful Land*, p. 47
92. *A Letter of Consolation*, p. 50
93. *In the House of the Lord*, p. 6
94. *In the Name of Jesus*, p. 22
95. *A Letter of Consolation*, p. 38
96. *The Way of the Heart*, p. 81
97. *With Open Hands*, p. 102
98. *Making All Things New*, p. 88
99. *A Cry for Mercy*, p. 139
100. *Love in a Fearful Land*, p. 34
101. *A Cry for Mercy*, p. 49
102. *The Road to Daybreak*, p. 169
103. *A Letter of Consolation*, p. 30
104. *Seeds of Hope*, p. 12
105. *The Way of the Heart*, p. 26
106. *Making All Things New*, pp. 74-75
107. *Making All Things New*, p. 65
108. *A Cry for Mercy*, p. 153
109. *The Road to Daybreak*, p. 5
110. *With Open Hands*, p. 126
111. *The Genesee Diary*, p. 37
112. *Seeds of Hope*, p. 102
113. *In the Name of Jesus*, p. 69
114. *The Genesee Diary*, p. 25
115. *With Open Hands*, p. 56
116. *Seeds of Hope*, p. 94
117. *The Way of the Heart*, p. 33

118. *Seeds of Hope*, p. 24
119. *Heart Speaks to Heart*, p. xiii
120. *The Wounded Healer*, p. 83
121. *A Cry for Mercy*, p. 41
122. *Reaching Out*, p. 54
123. *Reaching Out*, p. 54
124. *The Genesee Diary*, p. 39
125. *The Genesee Diary*, p. 42
126. *The Genesee Diary*, p. 87
127. *The Road to Daybreak*, p. 211
128. *Letters to Marc about Jesus*, p. 25
129. *The Genesee Diary*, p. 82
130. *A Letter of Consolation*, p. 51
131. *A Cry for Mercy*, p. 62
132. *The Wounded Healer*, p. 38
133. *The Road to Daybreak*, p. 188
134. *Reaching Out*, p. 54
135. *Seeds of Hope*, p. xvi
136. *The Road to Daybreak*, p. 22
137. *The Genesee Diary*, p. 13
138. *A Letter of Consolation*, p. 48
139. *The Genesee Dairy*, p. 63
140. *A Cry for Mercy*, p. 32
141. *The House of the Lord*, p. 20
142. *In the Name of Jesus*, p. 43
143. *Reaching Out*, p. 66
144. *Out of Solitude*, p. 40
145. *Seeds of Hope*, p. 5
146. *Reaching Out*, p. 59
147. *The Genesee Diary*, p. 133

148. *Seeds of Hope,* p. 23
149. *The Genesee Diary,* p. 106
150. *Seeds of Hope,* p. 46
151. *The Wounded Healer,* p. 38
152. *The Wounded Healer,* pp. 70-71
153. *The Genesee Diary,* pp. 144-145
154. *Seeds of Hope,* p. 17
155. *Reaching Out,* p. 49
156. *The Genesee Diary,* p. 119
157. *With Open Hands,* p. 120
158. *With Open Hands,* p. 94
159. *Seeds of Hope,* p. 37
160. *The Genesee Diary,* p. 85
161. *The Genesee Diary,* p. 48
162. *Seeds of Hope,* p. xiv
163. *Reaching Out,* p. 7
164. *With Open Hands,* p. 7
165. *In the Name of Jesus,* p. 10
166. *The Wounded Healer,* p. 91
167. *The Road to Daybreak,* p. 56
168. *Out of Solitude,* p. 55
169. *Letters to Marc about Jesus,* p. 14
170. *Out of Solitude,* p. 24
171. *The Wounded Healer,* p. 72
172. *The Genesee Diary,* p. 76
173. *Letters to Marc about Jesus,* p. 10
174. *Seeds of Hope,* p. 13
175. *The Genesee Diary,* p. 34
176. *The Genesee Diary,* p. 218
177. *Seeds of Hope,* p. 47

178. *Out of Solitude,* p. 41
179. *The Road to Daybreak,* p. 19
180. *Love in a Fearful Land,* p. 21

BIBLIOGRAPHY

Henri J. M. Nouwen, *With Open Hands*, Ave Maria Press, 1972

Henri J. M. Nouwen, *Out of Solitude: Three Meditations on the Christian Life*, Ave Maria Press, 1974

Henri J. M. Nouwen, *Reaching Out: The Three Movements of the Spiritual Life*, Doubleday, 1975

Henri J. M. Nouwen, *The Wounded Healer: Ministry in Contemporary Society*, Image Books, 1979

Henri J. M. Nouwen, *Clowning in Rome: Reflections on Solitude, Celibacy, Prayer and Contemplation*, Doubleday, 1979

Henri J. M. Nouwen, *In Memoriam*, Ave Maria Press, 1980

Henri J. M. Nouwen, *The Way of the Heart: Desert Spirituality and Contemporary Ministry*, Darton, Longman & Todd, 1981

Henri J. M. Nouwen, *The Genesee Diary: Report from a Trappist Monastery*, Doubleday, 1981

HENRI J. M. NOUWEN, Donald P. McNeil and
Douglas A. Morrison, *Compassion: A
Reflection on the Christian Life,*
Darton, Longman & Todd, 1982

HENRI J. M. NOUWEN, *Making All Things New,* Gill
& Macmillan, 1982

HENRI J. M. NOUWEN, *A Cry for Mercy: Prayers
from the Genesee,* Gill & Macmillan,
1982

HENRI J. M. NOUWEN, *A Letter of Consolation,* Gill
& Macmillan, 1983

HENRI J. M. NOUWEN, *The Living Reminder: Service
and Prayer in Memory of Jesus Christ,*
Harper & Row, 1984

HENRI J. M. NOUWEN, *Love in a Fearful Land: A
Guatemalan Story,* Ave Maria Press,
1985

HENRI J. M. NOUWEN, *In the House of the Lord,*
Darton, Longman & Todd, 1986

HENRI J. M. NOUWEN, *The Road to Daybreak: A
Spiritual Journey,* Doubleday, 1988

HENRI J. M. NOUWEN, *Letters to Marc about Jesus,*
Darton, Longman & Todd, 1988

HENRI J. M. NOUWEN, *Heart Speaks to Heart: Three
Prayers to Jesus,* Ave Maria Press,
1989

HENRI J. M. NOUWEN, *In the Name of Jesus:
Reflections on Christian Leadership,*
Crossroad, 1989

HENRI J. M. NOUWEN, *Seeds of Hope,* Robert
Durback (ed.), Darton, Longman &
Todd, 1989

HENRI J. M. NOUWEN, *Beyond the Mirror:
Reflections on Death and Life,*
Crossroad, 1990

HENRI J. M. NOUWEN, *Walk with Jesus: Stations of
the Cross,* Orbis, 1990

HENRI J. M. NOUWEN, *Life of the Beloved,*
Crossroad, 1992

HENRI J. M. NOUWEN, *Return of the Prodigal Son,*
Doubleday, 1992

HENRI J. M. NOUWEN, *Jesus and Mary: Finding Our
Sacred Center,* St. Anthony Messenger
Press, 1993

HENRI J. M. NOUWEN, *Our Greatest Gift: A
Meditation on Dying and Caring,*
Harper Collins, 1994

HENRI J. M. NOUWEN, *With Burning Hearts: A
Meditation on the Eucharistic Life,*
Orbis Books, 1994

HENRI J. M. NOUWEN, *Here and Now: Living in the
Spirit,* Crossroad, 1994

HENRI J. M. NOUWEN, *The Path of Waiting,*
Crossroad, 1995

HENRI J. M. NOUWEN, *The Path of Freedom,*
Crossroad, 1995

HENRI J. M. NOUWEN, *The Path of Power,*
Crossroad, 1995

HENRI J. M. NOUWEN, *The Path of Peace,*
Crossroad, 1995

HENRI J. M. NOUWEN, *Can You Drink this Cup?,*
Ave Maria Press, 1996

HENRI J. M. NOUWEN, *Bread for the Journey, A
Daybook of Wisdom and Faith,* Harper
Collins, 1996

HENRI J. M. NOUWEN, *The Inner Voice of Love: A
Journey through Anguish to Freedom,*
Doubleday, 1996

HENRI J. M. NOUWEN, *Adam: God's Beloved,* Orbis
Books 1997

HENRI J. M. NOUWEN, *Sabbatical Journey: The
Final Year,* Crossroad, 1997

INDEX

ABOUT THE AUTHOR

CHARLES RINGMA is an Australian trained at Reformed Theological College in Victoria. He holds degrees in divinity, sociology, and studies in religion. He has a Ph.D. in philosophical hermeneutics from the University of Queensland. He has served as a community worker among the Aborigines as well as the poor in Manila, and has lectured at Asian Theological Seminary. He established Teen Challenge in Australia. He is presently professor of missions and evangelism at Regent College, Vancouver.

HOW DOES YOUR FAITH STAND UP TO THE POWERS OF THIS AGE?

Resist the Powers

We live in busy times and find ourselves preoccupied with action and productivity. As a result, it is difficult to make time for prayer. Through a creative dialogue with Jacques Ellul, Charles Ringma invites you to cultivate a faith that resists the powers of this age.

Resist the Powers (Charles Ringma) $10

Seize the Day

Does your faith live inside church walls? This compilation of Dietrich Bonhoeffer's writings offers a look at the meaning of life and Christ in the world beyond church doors. Challenge yourself to move from the safety of the sanctuary into a troubled world that desperately needs the love of a savior.

Seize the Day (Charles Ringma) $10